IMAGES
of America

LOUISVILLE
in WORLD WAR II

IMAGES
of America

LOUISVILLE
in WORLD WAR II

Bruce M. Tyler
With foreword by
State Representative Darryl T. Owens

ARCADIA
PUBLISHING

Published by Arcadia Publishing
Charleston, South Carolina

Printed in the United States of America

Library of Congress Catalog Card Number: 2005932121

For all general information contact Arcadia Publishing at:
Telephone 843-853-2070
Fax 843-853-0044
E-mail sales@arcadiapublishing.com
For customer service and orders:
Toll-Free 1-888-313-2665

Visit us on the Internet at www.arcadiapublishing.com

I dedicate this book to my wife, Colleen Perry Tyler,
her mother, Barbara Perry Bradley,
my sister Deborah Tyler,
my youngest sister, Rosalind,
and her college-educated daughter, Donya.

CONTENTS

Foreword   6

Acknowledgments   7

Introduction   8

Bibliography   10

1. Louisville Goes to War   11

2. *Wings Over America* and Bowman Field   49

3. The First Troop Carrier Command   71

4. Special Bowman Field Base Activities   77

5. Base Recreation Activities   85

6. The 43rd Aviation Squadron at Bowman Field   93

7. Portraits of Soldiers   99

8. The Colored USO   107

9. Chickasaw Park and the Brock Building   115

10. Life in Company C at Bowman Field   119

FOREWORD

As a state representative to the Commonwealth of Kentucky, I strive to promote the general welfare of all Kentuckians. Legislation that serves the public should empower and enfranchise every individual citizen, regardless of race, socioeconomic status, religious affiliation, or sexual orientation. Without common rights, we have no common wealth. Laws, while imperative to protecting the citizenry, cannot engender a spirit of community by themselves. One of the best ways to achieve that spirit is to reflect on past struggles and triumphs, employing what we learn to impact the present and influence the future.

Reading Dr. Bruce Tyler's latest pictorial, *Louisville in World War II*, engenders the type of reflection that helps us re-envision Louisville cultural history. Rather than regurgitating propagandistic images that have come to typify depictions of the World War II era, Dr. Tyler's collection of archival photographs and documents depicts a multitude of Louisvillians doing war work during national distress. Across the pages, we see the many women and men who worked diligently to supply the Armed Forces with materials integral to military operations alongside teachers instructing their classes. Pictures reveal everyday people participating in daily activities like banking, shopping, and going to the movies, as well as planning dances and spending time with their families.

What is most salient about *Louisville in World War II*, however, is that it reveals the rarely documented contributions of Louisville's African American community to the war effort. Personal photographs that soldiers took while stationed here or visiting, as well as group shots that depict black troops working on specific projects, historicize a much neglected part of our cultural history. Including Louisvillians of many backgrounds highlights our indebtedness to a diverse Louisville community for keeping our city, state, and nation safe.

A career historian, Dr. Bruce Tyler has dedicated himself to making information and pictures that were once private, public. By making his works available to every citizen, Dr. Tyler has enriched the Louisville community and will enrich the nation at large. He is a public servant, urging us to remember, reflect, interpret, and employ what we learn from his collection of materials as we endeavor to build community based on what *Louisville in World War II* teaches us; this is our common history.

—Darryl T. Owens
State Representative

6

ACKNOWLEDGMENTS

In 1990, I met Mr. James Sydnor, who worked as a photographer from the 1920s to the 1970s. He had lost his many thousands of pictures in a basement flood at his home. He only had about 200 pictures left. I interviewed him and catalogued his pictures. He eventually died, but I had been bitten by the photograph-as-historical-document bug and thought it worthy work to salvage family and professional photographs and get them published.

Jefferson County Commissioner Darryl T. Owens had introduced me to James Sydnor and told me to work with him and others. Owens decided to fund a project to work in Louisville's African American history and supplied me with funding. He convinced Louisville city alderman Arthur Smith, a local minister of Portland Baptist Church, to join in and more importantly convinced me that I start working on a local history. They both had read Prof. George Wright's book, *Life Behind a Veil: Blacks in Louisville, Kentucky, 1865–1930* (1985). They were so impressed and wanted him hired at the University of Louisville, but he was rejected and he went elsewhere.

At the University of Louisville, there have been a few strong supporters of the Urban Mission—a program to research and help solve urban problems and illuminate urban history—mainly at the photographic archives, such as Delinda Stephen Buie, Susan Knoer, Bill Carner, and especially James (Andy) C. Anderson, who labored long hours for several months to bring to my attention the best photographs for this book on Louisville in World War II.

I wanted to remind Louisvillians of their glorious past and the crucial role that their people and institutions played in the world war and the absolutely vital role played by Bowman Field and its troops in winning the international fight for democracy and serving in the world's greatest international liberation army, the American military, despite its following the old Jim Crow racial patterns.

I received heroic help from Ada Lee Kane of Louisville, who rescued and brought to my attention, once again, the papers and pictures and life of Marguerite Davis, who served black troops at Bowman Field as their recreation director. Kane and relatives came to me, and Davis came herself to get involved once again and help preserve her work. Historian Charles Arrington introduced me to a lot of key information about Bowman Field to help make this book possible. I thank all the people who have worked to make this book possible. My debt is to the community people, like state representative Darryl T. Owens, who demanded that their history be recorded and published. I salute them and this is their history, *Louisville in World War II*.

Sincerely,
Dr. Bruce M. Tyler

INTRODUCTION

With the bombing of Pearl Harbor, the United States officially entered the European and Asian wars, or World War II. Wilson W. Wyatt Sr. of Louisville became mayor just at the start of the war in 1941. He was a New Deal Democrat and supporter of Franklin D. Roosevelt. He offered a 12-point program to modernize local government. He sought to equalize pay between men and women and blacks and whites. He intended to streamline city and county governments by eliminating any duplication of functions. He wanted to modernize redistricting so Louisville would get its full representation in the Kentucky State Legislature. Lighter financial burdens for the local people by modernizing the tax codes were his goal. He desired modern voting machines to eliminate voting corruption in elections. He thought that 10 percent of state funds for education must be set aside for the poorest districts. In short, he promoted a progressive agenda for the state of Kentucky and its premier city, Louisville.

As a result of the December 7, 1941, bombing of Pearl Harbor, the War Department called Mayor Wilson Wyatt and told him to post extra guards at Louisville area bridges that straddled the Ohio River. Extra guards were stationed at war plants. Louisville ranked number 18 as a war arsenal and was a vital link in the Arsenal of Democracy in the fight against Nazi Germany and Imperial Japan and Italy and their allies. Louisville was the major war plant hub, with a powder plant at nearby Charlestown and Rubbertown, and Louisville had major chemical plants producing wartime products. There was a major Naval Ordnance Plant and Ohio River shipyards. The Curtiss-Wright Aircraft industrial plant produced the emergency C-76 aircraft, which failed before mass production as a result of the weak wooden parts used before scrap metal campaigns made wooden parts unnecessary. Bowman Field held U.S. bomber squadrons. Also Fort Knox held the nation's gold supply. Louisville was a vital link, a strategic center of critical production, and a crossroads of transportation links on land and water and by air.

Mayor Wilson W. Wyatt spent half his time on war issues, war production, and rationing operations. He organized and chaired the Louisville Metropolitan Area Defense Council. It included Louisville and Jefferson County along with New Albany and Jeffersonville in southern Indiana located just across the Ohio River. Louisville was at the hub of this area's Arsenal of Democracy and the chief protector, planner, and operations center for regional defense as directed by the War Department. Mayor Wyatt called for 500 auxiliary police and another 500 firefighters, and he needed 1,000 air raid wardens. Nearly 6,000 (5,926) people volunteered for service. Over time, 50,000 people were involved as "citizen-volunteers." Wilson boasted, "The war emergency generated a spirit of close cooperation."

Wilson and his defense council spearheaded continuous scrap metal drives and aluminum metal and can drives to be smelted down and reused in war plants. Paper drives and war bond sales were promoted one after another without much letup. He and his group developed a war fund drive and supported the local USO and the Louisville Service Club that became a model for the nation for USO clubs. The defense council and other war-related agencies could dip into the war fund for their projects.

African Americans served as air raid wardens, and the black community was recruited into nearly every area of war work in war plants and in community service, including USO and

YMCA work and scrap metal campaigns. The defense council supervised rationing boards for tires, cars, gasoline, and food. Blacks served alongside white people on these boards under Wyatt's administration. Wyatt said there were rumors and fears that the "mixed"-race boards would not work and fall apart. The actual experience, said Wyatt, "worked exceedingly well." Louisville was the only city south of the Mason-Dixon line to racially mix its boards, and even Detroit officials inquired into Wyatt's methods, and Detroit is a far northern city and certainly among the largest centers of the American Arsenal of Democracy.

Mayor Wyatt boasted, "I appointed the first black member of the Board of Equalization, the first black member of the Library Board, and Louisville's Interracial Commission; doubled the number of blacks on the police force; and elevated the first black policemen to officers rank." He noted too that the Louisville Metropolitan Area Defense Council twice won the "Citation of Merit." *Life* magazine, in January 1944, held its "Life Goes to a Party" in Louisville at the famous Brown Hotel, and black rationing board members attended and joined the white members for the first time in the Brown Hotel ballroom for a social event.

Mayor Wyatt noted that some 60,000 soldiers served in nearby military camps such as Fort Knox and at Bowman Field. The Louisville Service Club and the USO provided a "Home Away from Home" for these soldiers. Victory gardens were encouraged, and citizens, schools, and military bases cultivated vegetables to increase the food supply and to help feed poorer families. Nutrition food shows and programs were promoted to keep war plant workers, students, and soldiers fit to "work, fight, or farm."

Kentucky's Churchill Downs in Louisville is the premier icon of the nation and world for horse racing, Thoroughbred horses, and the expert and meticulous breeding and training of horses. Nearly all race tracks shut down during the war. Martin J. Winn, the president and executive manager of Churchill Downs, approached Mayor Wilson W. Wyatt Sr. because he intended to keep the track open and wanted the help of the mayor. They struck a deal: keep the track open and donate a significant sum of money to the Louisville War Fund. They encouraged more local people to go the track and that everyone ride streetcars and not drive private automobiles to help rationing programs to save resources for the war effort. It worked. Mayor Wyatt proudly boasted, "The infield was occupied by tanks and exhibits from Fort Knox. The flavor was so completely changed that it became almost a civic and patriotic duty to go to Churchill Downs" with the knowledge that some of the profits went to the War Fund. This was no different than when Boxer Joe Louis fought Max Baer in January 1942 in Madison Square Garden in New York and donated his purse to the Navy Relief Fund. Sports and patriotism could go hand-in-hand. (See Wilson W. Wyatt Sr. *Whistle Stops: Adventures in Public Life*. Lexington: The UP of Kentucky, 1985; Bruce M. Tyler. "The Black Double V Campaign For Racial Democracy During World War II," (pp. 79–108) *The Journal of Kentucky Studies*, Vol. 8, September 1999; and Bruce M. Tyler. *From Harlem to Hollywood: The Struggle For Racial And Cultural Democracy*. New York: Garland Publishing, Inc., October 1992.)

BIBLIOGRAPHY

Arrington, Charles W. "Historic Bowman Field." *Friends Bulletin*, Vol. 11, No. 1, Spring 1988.

Bowman Bomber military and base newspaper.

Bowman Field Special Service News.

Crews, Clyde F. "Jitters: Louisville and World War II." *Louisville Magazine.* October 1989: 57–59.

Davis, Marguerite, interviewed by the author.

Kane, Ada Lee, interviewed by the author.

Kleber, John E., ed. *The Encyclopedia of Louisville.* "Abram Hite Bowman" (p. 107). UP of Kentucky, 2001.

The Louisville Courier-Journal.

The Louisville Times.

Microfilmed tapes, B2060 unclass(ified) 1626 and B2061 unclass(ified) 1945: Department of the Air Force, Air Force Historical Research Agency, Maxwell Air Force Base, AL. These tapes cover the Bowman Field wartime story or "Diary" of the base. The information, however, is especially uneven for the black unit stationed there. Tapes are in this writer's possession.

Peck, Edward. John E. Kleber, ed. *The Encyclopedia of Louisville.* "Bowman Field" (pp. 107–108). UP of Kentucky, 2001.

Porter, Marion. "Nurses with Wings." *Collier's.* April 22, 1944: 22–23, 69.

Sydnor, James, now deceased, interviewed by the author.

Tyler, Bruce M. *From Harlem to Hollywood: The Struggle for Racial and Cultural Democracy, 1920–1943.* New York: Garland Publishing, Inc., 1992.

———. "The Black Double V Campaign For Racial Democracy During World War II," *The Journal of Kentucky Studies*, Vol. 8, September 1999: (79–108).

U.S. Army Air Force. *Wings Over America: Bowman Army Air Base, Louisville, Kentucky; Army Air Forces Troop Carrier Command.* Washington, D.C. Air Forces Division, War Department, Bureau of Public Relations, *c.* 1944–1945.

Wyatt, Wilson Sr., now deceased, interviewed by the author.

Wood, Sandy. "Kentucky War Plants Set Record with 172,413 Employees in 1943." *The Louisville Courier-Journal*, January 1944: s-1, p. 10, col. 6–9.

The World War II Flight Nurses Association. *The Story of Air Evacuation, 1942–1989.* Dallas: Taylor Publishing Company, 1989.

One

LOUISVILLE
GOES TO WAR

With the bombing of Pearl Harbor on December 7, 1941, the nation, Kentucky, and Louisville mobilized as never before for full formal war to fight Nazi Germany and Imperial Japan. Citizens of all races and economic classes united in the effort both abroad and at home. Louisville's many industries banded together as well: the Mengel Company made wood products used in the war, and its staff burned a Nazi flag in an employee-held rally; Reynolds Aluminum Company manufactured arms and other war materials; Liberty National Bank sold war bonds at special windows; and the Louisville Ford Motor Company made at least 93,389 military jeeps out of the roughly 500,000 employed in the war. Louisville was an important industrial and military center and part of the Fifth Service Command area with surrounding states.

The 1940 U.S. Census revealed that Kentucky had a population of 2,845,000 people. Louisville's population numbered 319,077, and it ranked 25th in the nation among other cities in population. Also Kentucky war plants set a record employment level with 172,413 employees in 1943 according to the Federal War Manpower Commission, and it expected Kentucky to exceed that number in 1944. Louisville, needless to say, led the way as the most urban and industrial section of the state of Kentucky. The 172,413 war workers across the state included both men and women, and Louisville accounted for 102,000 of the workers. Twelve thousand war workers were added to the employment roles in 1942, or about 1,000 a month. Women accounted for 10,000 of those new workers across the state. Women numbered 47,487 war workers in Kentucky, and that number was expected to rise to 60,000 by May of 1944. The Louisville War Manpower director was Harry H. Hansbrough Jr., aged 32; he had reported for military service on February 2, 1944. Louisville ranked number 18 among American cities as a vital industrial and war plant center. In short, Louisville was the regional Arsenal of Democracy. (See "1940 Census Shows Wide Inequalities," *Louisville Courier-Journal*, March 30, 1941, s-3, p. 9, col. 6; John P. Marcum Jr., "Population," (714–715) in John E. Kleber, ed. *The Encyclopedia of Louisville*. Lexington: UP of Kentucky, 2001; Sandy Wood, "Kentucky War Plants Set Record With 172,413 Employees in 1943," *Louisville Courier-Journal*, January 2, 1944, s-1, p. 10, col. 6–9.)

The Mengel Company in Louisville was located at 1222 Dumesnil Street. At a July 4, 1944, celebration at the Fiber Container Department, management and employees burned a Nazi flag and hoisted the flag of the United States.

Shown here are students and their teacher at the Okolona Elementary School, a Louisville public school. This picture dated May 17, 1943, was made for the Central Dairy Council at 128 East Chestnut Street. It shows students how to eat healthy meals for sound bodies and minds as part of the home front effort to win the war. Note the slogan: "Victory Demands Healthy Americans."

This is an image called "Cadet Nurses lecture class" that was made for the Central Dairy Council on September 15, 1944. Cadets were taught nutrition and healthy foods for healthy living and how to provide services to those in or going into service. The United States learned from the border fights with Mexico's Francisco "Pancho" Villa that hygiene and healthy habits were crucial to keeping soldiers fit to fight.

This is a photograph of the factory interior of the Porcelain Metals Corporation, on May 15, 1942. Louisville was a vital center of war production and supplies for the Armed Forces during World War II. Note the slogan hanging on a banner: "YOU are a vital link in the chain of DEFENSE." Kentucky had 172,413 men and women war workers in 1943, and Louisville war workers comprised 102,000 of that number.

Pictured on July 9, 1942, is the exterior of the No. 7 plant at Third Street and Eastern Parkway of the Reynolds Metals Company. Reynolds provided materials used in the war. Note the slogan under the large billboard: "First in defense, first in peace."

This is a photograph made for the Curtiss-Wright Aircraft Factory Company's Employment Department on July 24, 1942, to show female students being trained in the machine shop at DuPont Manual High School in Louisville for war work. In 1943, women war workers in Kentucky numbered 47,487 compared to 37,174 in 1942. By May of 1944, their numbers were expected to rise to 60,000.

This is Reynolds Metals Company at 2500 South Third Street, and this reveals the interior of Plant No. 12 taken on June 18, 1943. They were producing parts for the war.

Pictured is the interior of a wartime factory plant of women war workers making military bags on an assembly line. This is at Meese, Inc., in Madison, Indiana, on May 2, 1945. This photograph was ordered by Zimmer Advertising Company as a publicity shot for the war work and women doing their patriotic duty.

This is an early photograph taken August 1, 1942, of woodwork at the Mengel Company of Louisville, showing wooden aircraft parts being made for the military. This woodwork was done out of fear of shortages of metal and aluminum. Scrap metal drives helped to fill the gap.

Shown here is another step in the production of wooden parts for the army air forces' arsenal of wartime plane parts. This work was being done at the Mengel Company in Louisville on August 1, 1942.

The nearly completed Mengel Company wooden aircraft part is shown here on October 22, 1942, at the aircraft division, which was located at 11th and Ormsby Streets in Louisville.

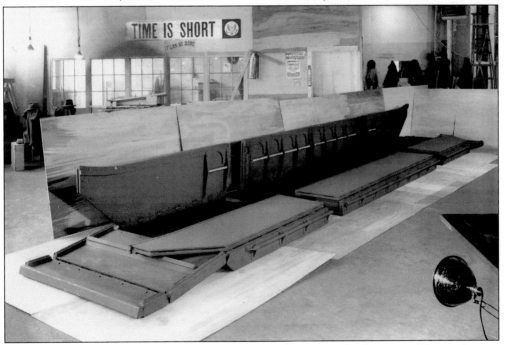

This is a folded pontoon made in Louisville on April 11, 1942, for Carpenter Houses, Inc., at 811–812 South Fifth Street in Washington, D.C.

Pictured on April 11, 1942, is the same unfolded pontoon made in Louisville for Carpenter Houses, Inc.

This photograph of the Louisville Ford Motor Company at 1400 South Western Parkway in the year 1942 or 1943 reveals the interior of the showroom picturing army trucks and commercial cars.

The Ford Motor Company showroom reveals army trucks and jeep and a commercial truck in 1942 or 1943. These vehicles were used in the Armed Forces.

Military jeeps and vehicles are loaded to transport by trucks to the railroad loading station at Louisville Bedding at 418 East Main Street in 1942–1943.

Central Trucking Systems, located at 1401 South Western Parkway, is shown here trucking military jeeps and vehicles to railroad cars for shipping out of Louisville to assigned locations for the war on August 13, 1945.

The Ford Motor Company noted this was the last military jeep produced at its Louisville plant as the 93,389th jeep. Louisville produced about one out of every five jeeps during the war in 1945.

On October 25, 1942, these aluminum workers were on a truck to pick up scrap metal that was to be reused in the war by melting it down and refashioning it for metal parts.

The Mengel Company, located at 11th and Dumesnil Streets, made this photograph on October 10, 1942, that shows men on a truck loaded with scrap metal with "Japan" written on the side sign. Reynolds Metals Company apparently melted scrap metal down to be used again in war material production.

In this Louisville service station scene are women attendants servicing cars. The Standard Oil Company had these pictures taken on December 8, 1942, to promote the war and to show that it was doing its part and employing women in jobs normally done by men.

Pictured here is a Standard Oil Company gas station with a woman attendant pumping air into a car tire. This was work normally reserved for men, except the wartime labor shortage led to recruiting women to work in this field. This gas station was located at 426 West Bloom Street.

The General Outdoor Advertising Company in Louisville made this war defense poster that was posted on the old Louisville Federal Post Office building located at Fourth and Chestnut Streets on September 29, 1941.

The Bourbon Stock Yards hosted a war bonds drive in 1942 among its employees and the public. It was quite common for businesses to sponsor war bond drives at the workplace.

The Seelbach Hotel is where the Bankers Meeting met in the spring of 1942 and promoted the sale of U.S. Defense Bonds.

At the yearly Kentucky State Fair, the American Red Cross put up a blood plasma center to collect blood for the soldiers of the Armed Forces as seen here on September 1, 1944. Sadly the blood of African Americans and Euro-Americans were kept separate based on outdated social conventions about race.

Uniformed women Red Cross workers in Louisville are raising money for the war effort in 1942. This was a popular activity for women.

This is a Buy War Bonds indoor booth with a uniformed Red Cross worker, Miss Utterbach, selling war bonds to other women at Stewart's Dry Goods Store on July 1, 1942. Note the wartime slogan: "Keep 'em Flying, Keep 'em Rolling, Keep 'em Sailing" to merge the home front battle with the battlefields abroad.

Shown here are a woman and baby in front of the war bonds window in the Liberty National Bank and Trust Company at Second and Market Streets on May 31, 1945.

Lined-up clerks stood at attention while the allied nations' national flags were hoisted at each window of the Liberty National Bank and Trust Company at Second and Market Streets.

This huge "Buy War Bonds" billboard stood in Louisville at the intersection of Brook and Broadway Streets. Billboards were a vital and effective way to get messages out to the public and were widely used in the war years.

On May 14, 1941, the General Outdoor Advertising Company held a food show that became a way to promote healthy eating habits during the war years as a defense measure.

This is a General Outdoor Advertising Company billboard with an Oertel Brewing Company moving display board saying, "Don't Let This Happen Here." This was an anti-Hitler and anti–German Nazi message to not let the Nazis enslave the world and the United States.

The M. R. Kopmeyer Company (advertising) displayed this duo-motion sign reading, "Buy War Bonds and Slappy Jappy." These catchy slogans were constant reminders that stayed in people's memories and reminded them who they were fighting the war against.

The Greater Louisville Building and Loan Association promoted this 1942–1943 display in shop windows in the downtown to attract the eyes and minds of shoppers. It showed images of bombs, a Revolutionary War minuteman statue, a poster of a minuteman, and a grave plaque and a machine gun as the centerpiece. The American flag was "The Emblem of Freedom: Now and Forever!"

This Victory show window display became common in downtown Louisville to mold and mobilize public opinion and get citizens to actively support the war in words and deeds. This image was taken on July 21, 1942.

Pictured is the Rialto Theater in Louisville with the marquee advertising the film *Hitler's Children* on January 15, 1943. In the movie, an American school in Berlin is next door to a school for the Nazi youth, and a bizarre plot ensues. In short, this was an anti-Nazi film.

This photo was made for Warner Brothers and shown at the Mary Anderson Theater in Louisville on August 18, 1942, to promote the film *Yankee Doodle Dandy*. Another display read, "On to Tokyo, All-Out Defense, We'll do Our Part." Another card advertised a war stamp and war bond rally held in the Henry Clay Hotel on August 18, 1942.

Singer and actor Bing Crosby (first row, second from left) posed for the camera with sailors and soldiers in Louisville in May 1942. Crosby left the Hollywood Victory Caravan in Houston, Texas, and came to Louisville to participate in an Army-Navy Relief Golf Tournament at the Audubon Country Club. Crosby and Bob Hope were to play together, but Hope could not make it, and Crosby played A. B. "Happy" Chandler (top row, far right). Crosby lost the match, but his golf club sold for $1,000.

Bing Crosby played golf in the May 1942 war relief golf match at the Audubon Country Club in Louisville. He and many other celebrities supported the war for freedom and peace.

Pictured is a Louisville World War II parade with a woman motorcyclist riding through downtown on Fourth Street in 1941–1942. On the reviewing stand are Mayor Wilson W. Wyatt and other military officers, probably from Fort Knox and Bowman Field where the army air forces' detachment squadron was based.

Shown here, another parade marches down Fourth Street in 1941–1942. The audience stands respectfully and applauds a marching band and majorettes that pass the reviewing stand. Mayor Wilson W. Wyatt and military officers from Fort Knox and Bowman Field review the marches.

The Billy Smith Sign Company and Associated General Contractors located at 633 South Fifth Street had this photograph made on November 11, 1942, of a parade float advertising the Shelter Construction Section of the Louisville Defense Council. Mounted on the float is a representation of an underground bomb shelter.

Here is a 1941 parade in Louisville with a float showing the earth, the U.S. flag planted in it, and a circle around the earth with the American wartime army air forces' production slogan, "Keep It Flying."

At Churchill Downs, normally famous for the Kentucky Derby and horse racing, area military troops were invited in 1942 to the race track to display their military weapons for the public and race fans. Troops are parading before the crowd as well.

Military WAACs (Women Army Auxiliary Corps) formed and marched at Churchill Downs in 1942. The presence of the troops at the racetrack projected images of war, defense, and patriotism.

Military WAACs are standing in formation at Churchill Downs during the racing season in 1942. These scenes merged horse racing with the war effort and showed horse racing as an all-American activity and a wholesome, healthy sport for citizens and soldiers alike.

Shown at Churchill Downs, military troops and their display of military hardware, weapons, jeeps, and tanks are mostly likely from Fort Knox and Bowman Field or perhaps Jeffersonville's Quartermaster Depot.

Two WAACs are shown at Churchill Downs during the races and military displays of war weapons and parading troops in 1942. Louisville's military bases included many women in military service.

Here, nearby Jeffersonville's Quartermaster Depot equipment is on display at Churchill Downs in 1942 along with other troops and WAACs at the racetrack. Churchill Downs, even during World War I, invited troops to hike there, let them in without charge, and gave them free iced tea.

Here is a Borden's milkman in a khaki-brown military-style uniform as a form of patriotic work dress and display. "Drink milk to help win the war by being healthy," seems to be the message.

This is the United Services Organization, or more commonly called the USO, headquarters in Louisville that served military men and provided "Your Home Away From Home." The Louisville USO opened on March 7, 1941. Note the large sign on the side of the building.

Louisville's USO became a model for the national USO operations across the country. This is a front picture of the Louisville USO headquarters at 525 South Fifth Street in downtown Louisville.

This USO picture on March 2, 1947, showed servicemen clustered around a USO hostess playing the piano. However, this was a typical World War II–era scene where female hostesses provided chatter, dancing, card playing, and entertainment for servicemen away from home.

This is the interior of the Louisville USO on March 17, 1942, when men are pictured reading and relaxing in a day room. The USO developed a whole program of recreational activities for soldiers. It had USO directors and assistance from the national level down to the local communities.

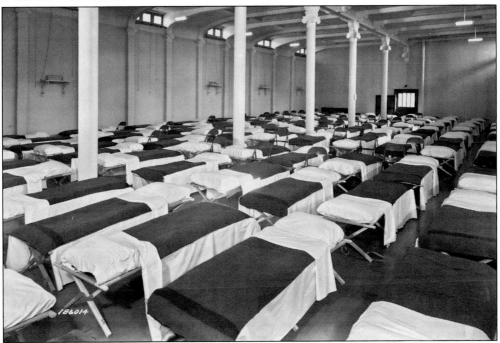

Pictured here on February 17, 1942, are beds in the USO dormitory located at 525 Fifth Street. The influx of soldiers was so large that a crisis soon developed because of a shortage of beds and places for soldiers to stay when off local bases. The USO provided some beds.

An unnamed couple, seen here on August 15, 1942, was at Fontaine Ferry, a very popular amusement park in Louisville. The man is an army air forces soldier. He was probably based at Bowman Field where the I Troop Carrier, the Glider Pilots Combat Teams, and Air Medical Evacuation Units were stationed and included pilots and flight engineers.

Pictured on March 17, 1942, are soldiers playing table tennis or ping-pong at the USO located in Louisville at 525 South Fifth Street. The USO established comfort buildings for soldiers' relaxation and wholesome recreation with supervision. The USO watchwords were: "A Home Away From Home."

These soldiers are playing billiards at the USO in Louisville. This was a popular pastime for soldiers based in the city. During one 30-hour period in World War II, 40,000 people visited the club.

This is a USO dance at their dance hall in the South Fifth Street headquarters. Dances were chaperoned, and "USO girls" were carefully screened and selected to maintain a wholesome environment and experience.

Pictured here is the interior of the USO Club with its lunch counter to serve breakfast and snacks and tables for reading, eating, and drinking coffee and beverages. Notice across the barrier is the sleeping quarters in this July 19, 1942, photograph. Louisville suffered from a severe shortage of beds for soldiers off of their bases. The USO expanded its beds to ease the problem and prevent the practice of soldiers sleeping in parks.

This is the interior lounge and reading room of the Louisville USO shown on July 19, 1942. This day room was typical of the USO; it gave soldiers a place to read, write letters, and chat with one another instead of hanging out in the streets, at pool halls or juke joints that sold alcohol, or around prostitutes that might have venereal diseases, which might injure soldiers' morals and health. Note the large picture of Gen. Douglas MacArthur on the rear wall.

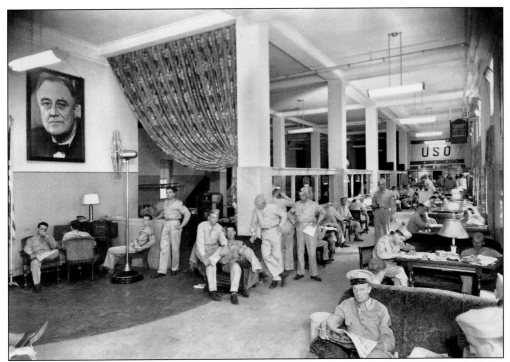

Seen here is the USO lounge and day room in Louisville at 525 South Fifth Street. Note the huge photograph of Pres. Franklin D. Roosevelt hanging in the room on July 19, 1942.

This is a picture of a soldier and his bride on February 6, 1944. This picture was made for A. Rosenberg at 2646 Portland Avenue. Some soldiers married local women they met while on duty in Louisville.

A soldier, his bride, bridesmaids, and groomsmen are shown here at Crescent Hill Baptist Church on December 21, 1943. Many soldiers married local women they met at the USO or in the Louisville area where they served during part of the wartime years.

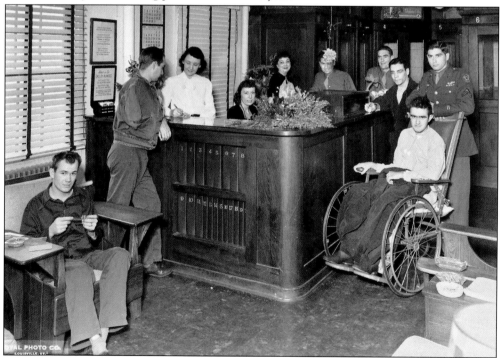

Shown here is a scene at Nichols Veteran's Administration Hospital on Christmas Day 1944. This hospital served military personnel and those returning soldiers who were sick or injured.

The Nichols Veteran's Administration Hospital, nurses, doctors, and recovering soldiers are seen in 1944–1945. The hospital served both white and black troops. Lena Horne, singer, dancer, and Hollywood actress, visited and performed at Nichols Hospital in 1944 or 1945, if not before.

Shown here is an outside scene at Nichols Veteran's Administration Hospital where patients recovered from injuries and sickness.

This image of Nichols Hospital on July 27, 1943, shows a garden party for sick and injured troops.

Here is a Louisville girl holding the Louisville *Courier-Journal* newspaper on August 14, 1945, with the headline screaming: "PEACE AT LAST!" VJ Day was a result of the surrender of Japan.

This is a post-1945 World War II scene on February 15, 1948, in Louisville at the Calhoun Amherst Company and construction site where company officials, employees, citizens, and soldiers participated in a flag-raising ceremony. The wartime spirit remains a vital factor in Louisville even now, as soldiers, veterans, and bases still exist there.

This parade in Louisville on Fourth Street downtown occurred in the post–World War II years. It shows a float with a globe and the words: "Kentuckians Serve The World Over in The United States Air Force." Kentuckians also had a glorious record from their service at Bowman Field during the war.

Louisville was a very informed and patriotic city in the post–World War II years. Pictured here are men of the Gideons International handing out Bibles and having a few words with a sailor and air force soldier about the benefits of the Bible, moral teachings, and the peace of the Christian faith.

Two

WINGS OVER AMERICA AND BOWMAN FIELD

Perhaps Louisville's most significant war contribution though was the use of Bowman Field as a U.S. Army Air Corps Detachment Squadron base. The I Troop Carrier Command was established in April 1942 and it remained at Bowman Field well into 1944. The I Troop Carrier Command units, the Air Medical Evacuation units, and the Glider Pilots Combat Training units all trained there. These specialized troops played an important role in saving lives at Normandy when large numbers of killed and wounded soldiers had to be evacuated out under fire. They were vital in winning the war and saving lives.

The Air Medical Evacuation units of medical surgeons and technicians included women nurses trained in combat wounds and medical care; they carried side-arms because they entered dangerous front lines to quickly retrieve and evacuate wounded and sick soldiers. The Medical Air Evacuation units retrieved soldiers from Normandy. Air power and planes in warfare were crucial in World War II. Air power was in its infant stage during World War I but had quickly matured and had multiple advantages never seen in warfare of the past. Air power quickened the pace of war and the distance of the battle fields were shortened by air transportation that allowed both supplies and combat soldiers to get the field of battle much sooner and make war more deadly. (See Sam Adkins, "Air Evacuation School At Bowman 'Paying Off'," *Louisville Courier-Journal*, July 31, 1944, s-1, p. 11, col. 3–4; "1st Troop Carrier Unit Celebrates 2d Birthday," *Louisville Courier-Journal*, April 30, 1944, s-1, p. 10, col. 1; Marion Porter, "Nurses With Wings," *Collier's*, April 22, 1944, 22–23, 69.)

The men and women of these specialized units were highly skilled and had to be able to learn quickly and be in excellent physical conditioning to perform their rigorous duties. Bowman Field had to quickly convert its facilities and the base area for this demanding training. In November 1940, Bowman Field got $420,000 for jobs and conversion and updating work at the base from the Works Progress Administration (WPA). (See "Bowman Field Gets $420,000 In W.P.A. Jobs, *Louisville Courier-Journal*, November 23, 1940, s-2.)

This is a city of Louisville aerial photo, and the Ohio River with Indiana is on the north side. Unseen Bowman Field was located a few miles southeast of downtown. Although this is a mid-1950s picture, it still represents a similar view of Louisville in the World War II years.

COMMONWEALTH OF KENTUCKY
UNITED WE STAND
DIVIDED WE FALL

BOWMAN FIELD

Land first owned by pioneer Col. John Floyd, later by German Baron von Zedwitz. Confiscated as alien property during World War I. Local businessman and aviation enthusiast Abram H. Bowman founded flying service with Robt. H. Gast on this site in 1920. Property purchased by City of Louisville in 1928 for development as municipal airport.

Presented by Ky. Aviation Association, Inc.

This is a Bowman Field historical plaque. Land was seized by the government from a German national when he joined the German military during World War I.

Bowman Field is pictured as a large open field prior to 1938. It was called "Bowman's cow pasture" because it was mainly a barren field yet to be developed and modernized.

In 1938, concrete runways were laid at Bowman Field to improve and modernize it and to accommodate newer, more powerful planes that needed longer and stronger runways. Also Bowman Field became the main supply center for Louisville and the surrounding environment after the disastrous 1937 flood. Dirt runways could be washed out and dangerous for planes landing, especially with heavy cargo.

Here is the main Bowman Field Administration Building located on the south side of the field. The building style was art deco. Most of the building was built under the auspices of the WPA, a New Deal program. The architect, builder, or engineer was Wischmeyer and Arrasmith, J. F., and Company, and the structure was built between 1929 and 1937. This photograph was taken by Bruce Tyler in 2003.

Pictured is the rear of the main Bowman Field Administration Building. At one point, an atrium stood atop the three-story central building section. This 2003 photograph is by Bruce Tyler.

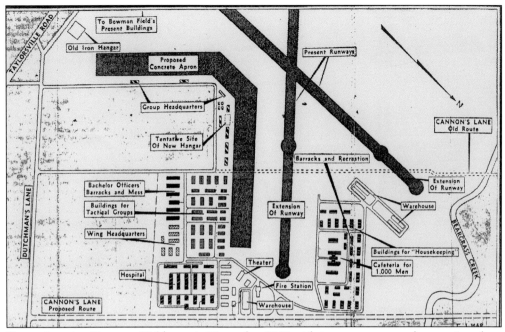

Shown here is a Bowman Field map in November 1940 with improvements and expansion plans to accommodate the influx of soldiers for wartime service, missions, and planes.

This is a book cover on Bowman Army Air Base, Louisville, Kentucky. This book is the most comprehensive snapshot of Bowman Field during the war years, and it was published by the U.S. Army Air Forces at Bowman Field. There were 3,277 men and women serving at Bowman Field on any given day in 1943 or 1944. The men constituted 68 percent of base personnel and women numbered 1,051 or 32 percent. Whites made up 92 percent of the base with African American men numbering 243 or 8 percent of the total. These numbers were tabulated by the author from the Army Air Forces Bowman Field annual book, *Wings Over America*, published in 1944.

This is the *Wings Over America* book published by the army air forces. The U.S. Army Air Forces spread its protective wings over America like a hawk to protect its people. The army air forces established its detachment squadron in the eastern section of Bowman Field.

A U.S. attack dive-bomber plane, the Vultee A-35 is shown here.

This is a foreword from the book *Wings Over America* in 1944 written by Gen. Henry H. Arnold, commanding general of the U.S. Army Air Forces.

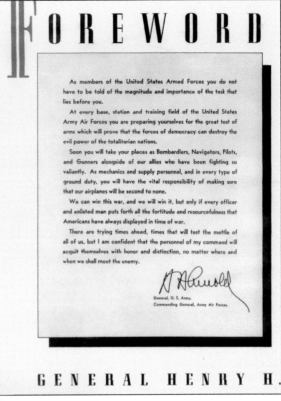

As members of the United States Armed Forces you do not have to be told of the magnitude and importance of the task that lies before you.

At every base, station and training field of the United States Army Air Forces you are preparing yourselves for the great test of arms which will prove that the forces of democracy can destroy the evil power of the totalitarian nations.

Soon you will take your places as Bombardiers, Navigators, Pilots, and Gunners alongside of our allies who have been fighting so valiantly. As mechanics and supply personnel, and in every type of ground duty, you will have the vital responsibility of making sure that our airplanes will be second to none.

We can win this war, and we will win it, but only if every officer and enlisted man puts forth all the fortitude and resourcefulness that Americans have always displayed in time of war.

There are trying times ahead, times that will test the mettle of all of us, but I am confident that the personnel of my command will acquit themselves with honor and distinction, no matter where and when we shall meet the enemy.

General, U. S. Army,
Commanding General, Army Air Forces.

GENERAL HENRY H.

Pictured here in 1944 is Gen. Henry H. Arnold, who led the U.S. Army Air Forces when the A-bomb was dropped on Japan.

The North Gate at Bowman Field.

Station Hospital Building.

HISTORY OF BOWMAN FIELD

Bowman Army Air Base, on the outskirts of the city of Louisville, Kentucky, is an important training base for the First Troop Carrier Command.

Bowman trained tactical units are serving today along the far-flung battle fronts in every theater of operations in World War II.

In June, 1942, shortly after the creation of the First Troop Carrier Command, Bowman Field came into the program of that Command.

Today, Bowman Field is a national headquarters of the famous Army Air Forces School of Air Evacuation, and every eight weeks this School turns out a class of Flight Nurses trained to evacuate the wounded from battle areas.

Troop Carrier groups, Airdrome Squadrons, the First Troop Carrier Command Replacement Center, the Glider Crew Training Center, and many other types of command activities have been based here.

Named for the late A. H. Bowman of Louisville, Bowman Field has worked in close coordination with the City of Louisville, and has cooperated on many projects of mutual interest.

Commanding Officers of the Base have been Colonel George P. Johnson, Colonel Tracy K. Dorsett, and Colonel Robert H. Wheat.

BOWMAN ARMY AIR FIELD HEADQUARTERS BUILDING

The history of Bowman Field is told through its buildings, and pictured are the North Gate (top left), the Station Hospital (top right), and the Headquarters Building. These were important elements of the base and its operations in 1944.

Pictured is a wartime hangar under construction at Bowman Field as part of major essential expansion of activities for the effective operation of the base. This photograph is by the War Department, U.S. Engineer Office. The Whittenberg Construction Company, general contractors, built temporary housing for Bowman Field in 41 days or by April 30, 1941, as an emergency war measure to expand the base. Some soldiers lived in tents until more barracks could be built.

The Army Air Forces School of Air Evacuation was located at Bowman Army Air Base.

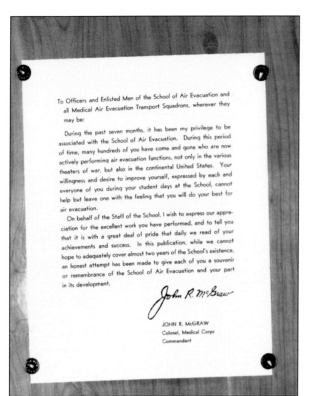

To Officers and Enlisted Men of the School of Air Evacuation and all Medical Air Evacuation Transport Squadrons, wherever they may be:

During the past seven months, it has been my privilege to be associated with the School of Air Evacuation. During this period of time, many hundreds of you have come and gone who are now actively performing air evacuation functions, not only in the various theaters of war, but also in the continental United States. Your willingness and desire to improve yourself, expressed by each and everyone of you during your student days at the School, cannot help but leave one with the feeling that you will do your best for air evacuation.

On behalf of the Staff of the School, I wish to express our appreciation for the excellent work you have performed, and to tell you that it is with a great deal of pride that daily we read of your achievements and success. In this publication, while we cannot hope to adequately cover almost two years of the School's existence, an honest attempt has been made to give each of you a souvenir or remembrance of the School of Air Evacuation and your part in its development.

John R. McGraw

JOHN R. McGRAW
Colonel, Medical Corps
Commandant

Pictured here is the wartime mission statement of John R. McGraw, colonel of the medical corps, that helped give identity, purpose, and direction to his troops and their wartime mission.

JOHN R. McGRAW
COLONEL

Commandant, School of Air Evacuation

John R. McGraw, colonel and commandant of the school of air evacuation, is pictured here with his biography notes that reveal his experience in the military.

58

HISTORY OF AIR EVACUATION

Colonel Stevenson, First Commandant of the School.

Often referred to as one of medicine's outstanding developments of World War II, Air Evacuation has expanded during World War II with the same speed that has marked the development of our "Astronomical" air force. Today it is saving lives and alleviating suffering on all of our far-flung fighting fronts.

Organized at Bowman Field, Louisville, Kentucky, on October 6, 1942, the first Air Evacuation training program was a realization of a dream which medical officers of the Army Air Forces had for many years to train Flight Surgeons, Flight Nurses and surgical technicians. It was still in the experimental stage when Major Scott M. Smith, then Commanding Officer of the School, and his staff of officers and nurses constantly sought new systems and ways to increase the speed and efficiency of the science of evacuation by air.

First known as the 349th Air Evacuation Group, and later redesignated the Army Air Forces School of Air Evacuation on June 25, 1943, and placed under the direct control of the Commanding General, Army Air Forces, this School has during its short history, trained numerous squadrons of officers, nurses and enlisted technicians who are now serving on all major battle fronts of the war.

Instrumental in the development of the School and its training program has been Colonel Ralph T. Stevenson, former Commanding Officer of the School, who assumed command of the organization soon after its establishment. Formerly a Dayton, Ohio, general physician, Colonel Stevenson received the rank of Lieutenant Colonel in December, 1942, and was promoted to the rank of full Colonel in October, 1943. He joined the Army in 1933 and after training

Lieutenant Elsie S. Ott, the first nurse to receive the Air Medal, is shown below receiving the award from Brigadier General Fred W. Borum, who made the presentation at Bowman Field.

Along with a brief history of air evacuation, Col. Ralph T. Stevenson (top left), Brig. Gen. Fred Borum, and Lt. Elsie Ott, who was the first to receive the Air Medal for her service, are pictured. The Air Medal is a graduation medal given when training is completed.

AT BOWMAN FIELD

at numerous Army Schools served in the Philippines from 1938 to 1940.

Present Commanding Officer of the School is Colonel John R. McGraw, 32, former Executive Officer, Surgeon's Office, Second Air Force Headquarters, Colorado Springs, Colorado, who relieved Colonel Stevenson on January 1, 1944. On that date, Colonel Stevenson was transferred to Headquarters, First Troop Carrier Command, Stout Field, Indianapolis, Indiana, where he assumed the duties of Command Surgeon.

An integral part of the program of the Army Air Forces School of Air Evacuation is the training of Flight Nurses, the Angels of Mercy who ride the skyways to care for the sick and wounded while in flight from battle zones to hospitals far behind the combat lines. A class of these nurses is now graduated from the School of Air Evacuation every eight weeks.

Today the Air Evacuation Nurse receives instructions in more than a dozen different courses which range from aircraft identification to oxygen indoctrination. Upon successfully completing this course she is presented with a diploma and a pair of gold wings which officially designate her as an Air Evacuation Nurse. Although numerous nurses were trained at the School of Air Evacuation and sent to active duty overseas prior to the establishment of a definite curriculum of study, the first class of nurses was not formally graduated until February 18, 1943.

The curriculum at the school is designed to acquaint the three classes of personnel involved—flight surgeons, flight nurses and enlisted men of the Medical Department—with their special responsibilities for administering emergency medical treatment, classifying patients, loading patients on the plane, and treatment while in the air. Training courses are carried along concurrently for each of these three groups so that, at the conclusion of the training period, complete tactical organizations with their complement of doctors, nurses, and enlisted personnel are ready for assignment to overseas duty.

The curriculum of the School has been set up with one primary purpose: to equip each nurse for the vital hours she spends in the plane. All the courses are practical.

Core of the Flight Nurse's course is training in subjects that specially pertain to her work under flying conditions. Her instructors at the School are Flight Surgeons—graduates of the School of Aviation Medicine at Randolph Field, Texas, which has long been famous for its experimentation with the effects of flying on the human body. Effects of high altitude on a patient's condition must be taken into account; dosage of certain medicines must be increased; others sharply reduced.

The activities of the School of Air Evacuation and its comprehensive training program has attracted international notice and

THE COLOR GUARD

acclaim. Many prominent personages have visited the School to inspect its training curriculum. These include Mrs. Franklin D. Roosevelt, General H. H. Arnold, Commanding General of the Army Air Forces, Senora Anesia Machado, Brazilian aviatrix, and Lieutenant Colonel Nellie V. Close, Chief Nurse in the Air Surgeon's Office.

Latest figures released from Army Air Forces offices show that 250,000 casualties from every major theater of operation have been successfully evacuated since the outbreak of the war. Playing no small role in this vital function have been the hundreds of pretty, competent Lieutenants of the Army Nurse Corps whose names appear on the following pages of the history of the Army Air Forces School of Air Evacuation at Bowman Field.

Lieutenant Ruth M. Gardiner of Indianapolis, Indiana, was the first nurse to be killed in a theater of operation in this war. Lieutenant Gardiner graduated from Philadelphia General Hospital in 1935.

First Lieutenant Burton A. Hall was the first flight surgeon from the School of Air Evacuation lost in action in the South Pacific area. Lieutenant Hall graduated from Hahnemann Medical School in 1938.

At Bowman Field are pictured a four-man color guard, Lt. Gardiner, and Lt. Burton Hall as they engage in military affairs at the base.

Shown is a Bowman Field base ceremony with Gen. Junius W. Jones presiding as a military medal is awarded to Pvt. Llewellyn G. Alter Jr. for his heroic action to save lives of pilots in a crash at Langley Field, Virginia, on March 6, 1941.

Chester C. Doherty (top row), first lieutenant colonel and assistant commandant of the School of Air Evacuation, and, from left to right, Captains Edwin McBride and John Horton and Maj. Russell Smith are pictured. They played crucial roles in making Bowman Field a success story by effectively training troops.

CHESTER C. DOHERTY
Lieutenant Colonel
Assistant Commandant of School of Air Evacuation

EDWIN J. McBRIDE
Captain
Deputy of Administration and
Services

JOHN J. HORTON
Captain
Deputy of Supply and
Maintenance

RUSSELL C. SMITH
Major
Director of Training

[60]

Snapshots of School of Air Evacuation

Left to right: General H. H. Arnold, left, conferring with General D. N. W. Grant, Colonel E. L. Bergquist and Colonel R. T. Stevenson after inspecting the School of Air Evacuation at Bowman Field on May 5, 1943.

Brigadier General Grant, left, Air Surgeon of the Army Air Forces, talks things over with Brigadier General E. G. Chapman, commanding general of the Airborne Troops, at the first graduation of nurses at Bowman Field, February 26, 1943.

Ceremonies presenting Air Medal to Second Lieutenants Gerda Bouwhuis, Seraphine Petrocelli and Regina Brown. Colonel Stevenson and Lieutenant Colonel McGraw made the presentation.

Loading demonstration in honor of General Arnold.

Colonel Ralph T. Stevenson, left, and Lieutenant Colonel John R. McGraw (right) welcome back to Bowman Field three nurses who have returned from active duty in the South Pacific. From left to right, the nurses are Lieutenants Regina Brown, Seraphine Petrocelli and Gerda H. Bouwhuis.

Mrs. Franklin D. Roosevelt is escorted on her inspection of the School of Air Evacuation by General Grant and Lieutenant Colonel McGraw.

Here are snapshots of the School of Air Evacuation with commentary and six photos, including Eleanor Roosevelt, the president's wife, at Bowman Field on January 27, 1944.

Pictured are Maj. Gen. David N. W. Grant (left), air surgeon, and Lt. Col. John R. McGraw (third from left), commanding officer of AAF School of Air Evacuation, with Eleanor Roosevelt being interviewed by a reporter at Bowman Field. Roosevelt visited Bowman Field on January 27, 1944, to view the female nurses and the facilities. Roosevelt was justly proud of these women who, like the men, entered the forward combat zones to retrieve wounded soldiers to get them to safety and recovery as soon as possible by risking their lives. Roosevelt said of the nurses and facilities that they were "excellent."

Pictured is a B-17 plane with Gene Autry on board when he visited Bowman Field. Autry was a popular film star who played cowboy roles.

Colonel John R. McGraw.

Above: High Army officials review the School of Air Evacuation on the event of its first anniversary.

★

Right: Canadian nurses and officers of the Royal Canadian Air Force completed the course at the School of Air Evacuation at Bowman Field, graduating with the seventh class. Shown, left to right, are Nursing Sisters Lack, LaBreque, Collings, Jorgensen, Hardwick, Pinckney, and Flight Lieutenants Lloyd-Smith and Nonnamaker.

★

Below, left: Instructing at bivouac with the fourth class are, left to right, Captain Edward Phillips, Lieutenant Leora B. Stroup, Captain William P. McKnight, Second Lieutenant Andrew F. Gruber, Captain Andrew D. Henderson, Captain Edward A. Sawan, and First Lieutenant Joseph A. Alfieri.

Below, right: The Flight Training Office.

This is an air evacuation photo collage of five pictures from 1943–1944, including, from top to bottom and left to right, air evacuation's first year, Col. John R. McGraw, flight nurses, pilots and field training, and flight training officers. These were highly skilled soldiers who trained for operations packed with high danger and risk taking. Bowman Field operations were vital to the country's war effort and making troops combat-ready.

BIVOUAC

Explaining the compass during bivouac of the fourth graduating class (upper left) are, left to right, Lieutenant Colonel Stevenson, Second Lieutenants Mary R. Svahula, M. Elizabeth Binkley and Beatrice E. Roberts. During bivouac one may expect to crawl through the most inaccessible places (upper right). There are no beauty parlors on bivouac. The girls shown at the lower left are not priming for dates. The idea is to make oneself look as much as the surrounding terrain as possible. Hard work brings on a tremendous thirst, and the old lister bag (lower right) comes in handy. Coca-Cola wasn't there that time, but the good old drinking water was.

The Air Evacuation nurses line up for inspection (upper left). A different bu t more popular lineup is that for mess (upper right). During a lull in the seventh inning, the nurses indulge in the pause that refreshes (lower left). During off-moments a popular place with nurses is the Post Exchange (lower right).

Shown here are the bivouac, photographs on and off the field, and commentary about Bowman Field troop activities that were vital to their work and well-being as they tried to stay fit to fight in 1943–1944.

NURSING SERVICE

MARY R. LEONTINE Major	LEORA B. STROUP Captain	ANNE M. BARAN Captain	AVA A. MANESS Second Lieutenant
AGNES A. JENSEN Second Lieutenant	HELEN PORTER Second Lieutenant	EUGENIE H. RUTKOWSKI Second Lieutenant	VIRGINIA C. DEIBEL Second Lieutenant

★ ★

DEPARTMENT OF TRAINING

LAURENCE L. PALITZ
Major

LEO S. BELL Captain Instructor	MILTON GREENBERG Captain Instructor	GEORGE H. GRAY Major Air Convoys Liaison Officer	PAUL C. MALL Captain Instructor	ANDREW F. GRUBER Captain Instructor	WILLIAM V. MAYER First Lieutenant Instructor

★ **S T A F F** ★

WARREN H. HINTZ Captain Personnel Officer	HOWARD F. PHILLIPS First Lieutenant Adjutant	JEAN H. WERTHER, JR. First Lieutenant Detachment Commander	SOLOMON SHIFF First Lieutenant Mess Officer	HAROLD JAFFREY First Lieutenant Supervisor of Supply	HENRY F. OTTER First Lieutenant Assistant Personnel Officer

The Nursing Service and Department of Training program provided vital wartime training and services to the United States's war efforts and final victory. The work of the female combat nurses was so dangerous that they were trained in side-arms, which they wore in case they encountered enemy soldiers in forward combat zones while retrieving wounded soldiers.

CLASSES

Classroom work keeps them occupied for a considerable portion of the time during the courses at the School of Air Evacuation at Bowman Field. Many and varied are the subjects covered, and all tend to condition the pupils for the circumstances they will face on the flying fronts. Nurses are briefed before flight (upper left); trained in a mock plane to attend wounds during flight (upper right); given the old one-two-three for added pep (lower); instructed in the proper manner in which to load casualties (center); and are taught to identify planes immediately upon sight (bottom).

Below: Unloading ambulance plane.
Lower: Nurses march after retreat parade.

Shown here are classes of the air medical evacuation units at Bowman Field and their training and exercise. These classes often lasted eight weeks, and then other classes were brought in for training and rotated out as new ones came in.

The Flight Surgeon's Oath

I accept the sacred charge to assist in the healing of the mind as well as the body.

I will at all times remember my responsibilities as a pioneer in the new and important field of aviation medicine. I will bear in mind that my studies are unending; my efforts ceaseless; that in the understanding and performance of my daily tasks may lie the future usefulness of count less airmen whose training has been difficult and whose value is immeasurable.

My obligation as a physician is to practice the medical art with uprightness and honor; my pledge as a soldier is devoted to Duty, Honor, Country

I will be ingenious. I will find cures where there are none; I will call upon all the knowledge and skill at my command. I will be resourceful; I will, in the face of the direst emergency, strive to do the impossible.

What I learn by my experiences may influence the world, not only of today, but the air world of tomorrow which belongs to aviation. What I learn and practice may turn the tide of battle. It may send back to a peacetime world the future leaders of this country.

I will regard disease as the enemy; I will combat fatigue and discouragement as foes; I will keep the faith of the men entrusted in my care; I will keep the faith with the country which has singled me out, and with my God.

I do solemnly swear these things by the heavens in which men fly.

Flight Nurses's Creed

I will summon every resource to prevent the triumph of death over life.

I will stand guard over the medicines and equipment entrusted to my care and ensure their proper use.

I will be untiring in the performance of my duties, and

I will remember that upon my disposition and spirit will in large measure depend the morale of my patients.

I will be faithful to my training and to the wisdom handed down to me by those who have gone before me.

I have taken a nurse's oath reverent in man's mind because of the spirit and work of its creator, Florence Nightingale. She, I remember, was called the "lady with the lamp."

It is now my privilege to lift this lamp of hope and faith and courage in my profession to heights not known by her in her time, — Together with the, help of flight surgeons and surgical technicians, I, can set the very skies ablaze with life and promise for the sick, injured and wounded who are my sacred charges.

...This I will do, I will not falter, in war or in peace.

David N.W. Grant
Major General, U.S.A.
Air Surgeon

The Flight Surgeon's Oath and the Flight Nurses's Creed are printed here. They were written by David N. W. Grant, major general and air surgeon at Bowman Field. These creeds were part of the vital understanding of their work and wartime mission to literally save the world from mass murder, genocide, and destruction by the Axis powers.

Training classes were conducted on the proper methods to carry the sick and wounded soldiers onto an air evacuation plane. Trainees had to learn to treat injured patients and move them quickly and with care to avoid further injury and pain.

These medical personnel were training on loading and securing wounded soldiers onto medical bunks on planes and strapping them in for their safety while in flight.

Women who have earned their "Wings for Flying Nurses"—a metal pennant awarded upon graduation from military training—are pictured during a graduation class in V-formation in front of an air medical evacuation plane. V is for victory.

Graduation day finds them eager and ready to go on their first mission. Shown, upper left, flight nurse and surgical technician simulate the evacuation of wounded from the battle zone. Flying nurses go on the air in more ways than one (upper right), while others, in flying togs, scan the horizon with maps in hand (lower left). A nurse cuts her cake while they sing "Happy Birthday" (center), while another proudly displays her wings (lower right).

The nurse fully realizes the importance of discipline in Army life as she stands rigidly for inspection.

Wings fo[r]

Four riotous weeks of training ended, gold Flight Nurse's wings were waiting for these nurses, the first official air evacuation group graduated from Bowman Field, as they were told to prepare for immediate call to foreign duty. Flying nurses wear flying togs, but her hospital uniform is the traditional white dress.

Shown here is training, graduation, and the awarding of "Wings for Flying Nurses." This was a proud day for these medical technicians, who would provide a vital and life-saving service to combat troops in forward zones of fighting by bringing them out for further medical care after emergency battlefield medical care.

Three

THE FIRST TROOP CARRIER COMMAND

The I Troop Carrier Command was based at Stout Field in Indianapolis, Indiana, and it had a vital detachment and training unit based at Bowman Field in Kentucky. Bowman Field in April 1942 hosted the units rotating into and out of Bowman Field for their training. The slogan of the I Troop Carrier Command was "They Get There First" because of their air transport on C-47s. These planes carried cargo and combat-ready troops. Airplanes provided both speed and delivery of firepower and supplies to the battlefields. Brig. Gen. Frank W. Evans commanded the Stout Field I Troop Carrier Command, and units at Bowman Field were under his command as well with local base commanders.

These units had attached to them the glider pilot combat units that also trained at Bowman Field. These were paratroopers trained to get to the battlefields quickly by air transport and by flying in gliders held in tow behind C-47 transport planes. When landed, these troops scrambled to the turf combat-ready, and they landed near or up to the front lines of combat for ready action. These troops and pilots had to train to operate in direct line of danger and difficult tasks. Pilots had to learn to not only fly, but to tow glider planes behind the C-47s filled with paratroopers. These troops had to practice this skill and to be able to tolerate rough landings and come out ready for combat. The glider pilot combat unit training was rough and demanding. They learned to jump into burning water soaked in gas and oil and swim to safety, as shown in one of the pictures. They were expected to land in the war zone and be ready for combat.

The I Troop Carrier had to adapt to multiple tasks during the war. They flew supplies, troops, and nurses to the front lines and took the wounded and sick troops out. At Bowman Field, the glider pilot training units were excellent in sports at the base, but the African American 43rd Aviation Squadron was the only unit to beat them twice in softball games in 1943. (See U.S. Army Air Forces, *Wings Over America*, Louisville, Bowman Field, 1944.)

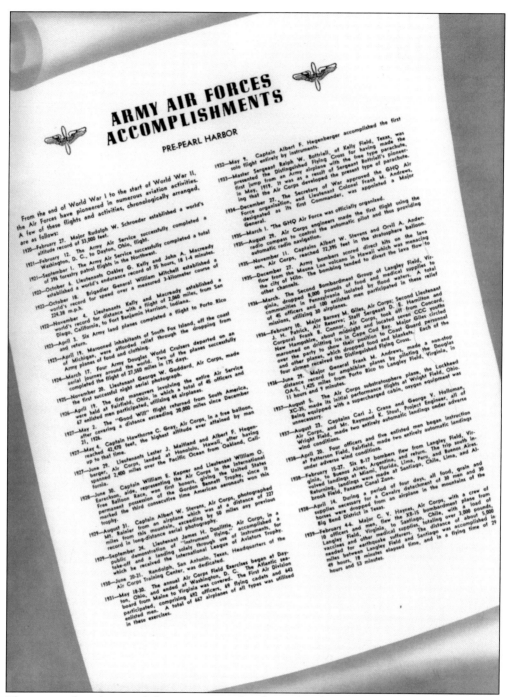

The army air forces' accomplishments are noted in this outlined history beginning with a pre–Pearl Harbor dateline. Air power became more and more vital to modern warfare, and Louisville's Bowman Field was part of the cutting edge of this new air power.

Pictured is Brig. Gen. Frederick W. Evans, commanding general of the first troop carrier command at headquarters at Stout Field, Indiana. Bowman Field was part of his extended operations.

HEADQUARTERS
FIRST TROOP CARRIER COMMAND
STOUT FIELD, INDIANA

★

The I Troop Carrier Command, organized April 30, 1942, has grown from fifty converted airliners and a handful of pilots until it is now bigger than the whole U. S. Army Air Forces of these years ago.

Youngest of the AAF's major branches, its officers and men today can look back with pride on the record it has made. Troop Carriers are now serving in every combat theater on the globe.

Troop Carrier units have piled up a formidable list of "first arrivals." Dropping paratroopers and gliders, they have furnished the spearhead of invasion in Africa, in Sicily, and in the South Pacific. An American Troop Carrier plane came to a halt on a captured airfield at Munda, in the Russell Islands, just as the Japs were retreating over the hill.

After successfully delivering combat troops in every war zone, Troop Carrier planes have flown back to the front countless times with supplies for the fighting men of the ground forces. On their return trips they have carried the wounded. So far, over 200,000 casualties have been flown by the TCC from battle areas to base hospitals, saving countless lives.

All of this has not been accomplished by accident. It was achieved by the hard work, fortitude and resourcefulness of every officer and enlisted man in the organization.

To the personnel of the I Troop Carrier Command serving in this country and to Troop Carrier units all over the world, this book is gratefully dedicated.

FREDERICK W. EVANS
Brigadier General, U. S. A.
Commanding

Pictured here is General Evans's commentary document on the mission of the first troop carrier and the statistical record of its accomplishments.

Pictured is the "Glider Drivers Under Aerial 'Rule of Thumb.'" This was carried in *The Bomber*, a military newspaper, at Bowman Field on June 1, 1943. This is a picture of what the glider pilots' plane and glider looked like.

Shown are soldiers jumping into burning water, which simulated combat and glider plane crashes and how to handle the emergency at the Bowman Field Glider Pilot Training School at the base. Landing Ship Tank (LST) crews also trained in this manner in 1943–1944.

TROOP CARRIERS LAND PARATROOPERS IN MARKHAM VALLEY, NEW GUINEA

THE STORY OF THE FIRST TROOP CARRIER COMMAND

When airborne troops were activated by the Army, the need for a specialized branch of the Army Air Forces to fly them into battle became apparent.

The result was the organization of the I Troop Carrier Command on April 30, 1942. Its original mission was to transport the airborne troops, but many other missions have been added.

Today, it not only carries airborne infantry and drops paratroopers. It also pilots the gliders, evacuates wounded soldiers from the battlefields,

Glider troops load up.

Here are photographs and an article called "The Story of The First Troop Carrier Command" detailing its history in war and peace.

keeps supplies flowing to fighting troops at the front, and transports the airborne engineers.

To the headquarters at Stout Field, Indianapolis, Indiana, were added training bases in eight states. From them the Troop Carrier Command has sent planes, pilots and crews all over the world.

This newest of Army Air Forces organizations has introduced into modern warfare a new technique, the effects of which are being felt from the icy islands of the Aleutians to the sultry sands of the South Pacific.

It was the Troop Carriers that landed the first American paratroopers in Africa after a 1,500-mile nonstop flight from England to Oran; it was the Troop Carriers that spearheaded the attack in Sicily and landed paratroopers in the thick of the fighting at Salerno. Troop Carriers evacuated thousands of wounded Marines at Guadalcanal, landed supplies to troops fighting at Munda and on the Russell Islands and at Bougainville. At most of these places, the Troop Carrier Command landed the first Allied plane, frequently almost before the fighting subsided.

They needed an infantry division—that's over 10,000 men—in Port Moresby and the 600 miles of sea from Australia was full of Jap ships. The Troop Carriers got it there.

A chaplain stationed in North Africa has described the Troop Carriers thus:

"They are the freight-pushers and taximen of the Air Corps. Their pilots are not only good. They are marvelous.

"They would fly a barn door, if outboard motors were attached, take off in a rainstorm, deliver a payload to Hell's front doorstep, thumb their nose at the devil and scoot back for another trip."

Air evacuation of the wounded by the Troop Carrier Command is one of the outstanding achievements of this war.

The first overseas evacuation unit was set up in North Africa. Wounded Americans and Tommies were flown from the battlefront back to rear bases for treatment. Similar units later were used in Sicily, Italy, and are now in use in the South Pacific.

In many major battles, ground troops have been solely dependent upon the Troop Carrier Command for supplies to keep them fighting for days. This was true at Bougainville, at Munda and on Guadalcanal.

Airborne aviation engineers, flown to the scene, have cut landing strips through deserts and jungles and have built fields in every theater of operation.

To enumerate the incidents of heroism displayed by Troop Carrier pilots, crews and supporting personnel would take many pages. The list of citations is long.

"They get there first" is the motto of the Troop Carrier Command. They are living up to it throughout the world.

To the Right, Top: Parapacks loaded with food go into plane. Center: Troop Carriers supply British VIII Army. Bottom: Wounded British Tommies are evacuated by air in North Africa.

Noted here are photographs of a troop carrier plane and the story of its activities in war.

Four

SPECIAL BOWMAN FIELD BASE ACTIVITIES

A few years before the war, Bowman Field was expanding and modernizing its facilities under the Works Progress Administration. After Pearl Harbor, it quickly became a fully functional base for the troops who served there. The base was altered to fit the needs of the troops and to train them for their specialized missions. Bowman Field built a base telegraph office to handle the flow of information and war secrets. The base built a typical military religious chapel for all to use no matter race, creed, or color. All were welcome at the chapel. Other military office workers handled mail and communications for the base and for the men and women serving there. Military Police served the base, and they did not have many problems because the troops were generally disciplined, orderly, and too busy for rowdy conduct. The base boasted of a photographic lab and printed and published a base newspaper that included photographs of base activities. The base had medical doctors, staff, and facilities to treat soldiers who had suffered battlefield wounds, who simply got sick on base, or who acquired sexually transmitted diseases. Some troops caught the measles and the mumps and were treated. (See "Mumps and Measles Hit Bowman Air Base," *Louisville Courier-Journal*, March 1, 1941, s-1, p. 3, col. 5; and U.S. Army Air Forces, *Wings Over America*, Louisville, Bowman Field, c. 1944.)

The base had a full medical department, dental, and optometry to treat soldiers in need of care. Good health care was part of the normal human services the military provided to keep soldiers healthy and "fit to fight" and to keep their morale up by offering the best medical care available to them on and off the battlefield. The photography lab made pictures and put them in the base newspapers to show the activities of the troops in their leisure time and base dances and events to keep their morale up. Bowman Field had WAACs on base to support the troops and to serve their country in time of war. In fact, Bowman Field had a large number of women in the specialized field of combat nursing. (Ibid.)

ROUND THE FIELD

"Please send ten dollars." . . . Many messages begin like this at the Base Telegraph Office.

Round the Field buildings and activities are pictured in 1944, including the base telegraph office and the library.

In 1944, religious service conducted in the field and the chapel was open to all, despite race, creed, or gender. The rigid racial segregation system in place throughout Louisville and at Bowman Field was not enforced at the chapel on base.

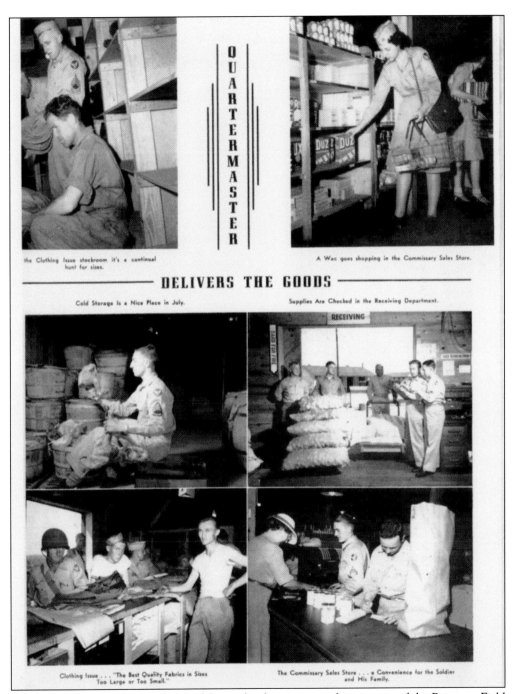

QUARTERMASTER

the Clothing Issue stockroom it's a continual hunt for sizes.

A Wac goes shopping in the Commissary Sales Store.

DELIVERS THE GOODS

Cold Storage Is a Nice Place in July.

Supplies Are Checked in the Receiving Department.

RECEIVING

Clothing Issue . . . "The Best Quality Fabrics in Sizes Too Large or Too Small."

The Commissary Sales Store . . . a Convenience for the Soldier and His Family.

Pictured are base supplies and their delivery for the necessary functioning of the Bowman Field Air Base and for the several thousand men and women based there at any given time. Shown is a commissary for the troops to shop at on base.

Service is the watchword with Military Police. With them lies the responsibility of maintaining order and guarding the installations at Bowman Field with the courtesy and discipline that characterizes the American Army.

Military Police Ride Jeep on Routine Patrol.

Military Police

Tabulating Reports at the Main Gate.

The Sunset Gun Fired at "Retreat" by Military Police.

The military police and some of their basic duties at the base are covered in this image. The staff and military personnel at Bowman Field were generally orderly and well disciplined.

MEDICAL OFFICERS

★  ★

SIDNEY M. EVANS
First Lieutenant
Medical Supply Officer

PETER G. KUTRA
Captain
Medical Officer

LEON LEDERKRAMER
Captain
Dental Officer

LAWRENCE LIEBERMAN
Captain
Dental Officer

HOMER J. SCHOLL
Captain
Dental Officer

CHESTER C. STEVENS
Captain
Dental Officer

MEYER H. LEVINE
First Lieutenant
Convalescent Training Officer

VELMA G. DAVIS
First Lieutenant
Chief Nurse

C. M. DONNELLY
Second Lieutenant
Nurse

ELIZABETH A. DUVALL
Second Lieutenant
Nurse

DORIS M. DWYER
Second Lieutenant
Nurse

MARY T. FINNERTY
Second Lieutenant
Hospital Dietitian

DOLORES E. HILL
Second Lieutenant
Nurse

CHARLOTTE M. JOHNSON
Second Lieutenant
Nurse

VERNA MEADE
Second Lieutenant
Nurse

HELEN A. MEEKER
Second Lieutenant
Nurse

DOROTHY B. WITCHER
Second Lieutenant
Nurse

[40]

The medical officers at Bowman Field were to keep the men and women there healthy and strong so they could defend America. They helped train medical technicians in the arts of combat medicine techniques in 1943–1944.

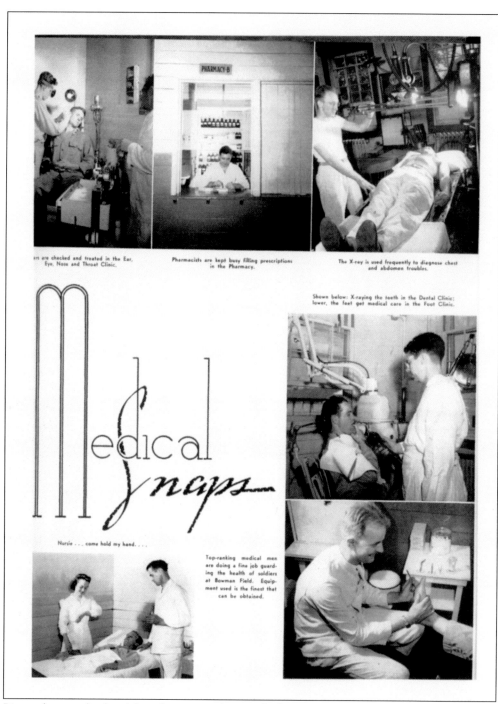

Medical Snaps

are checked and treated in the Ear, Eye, Nose and Throat Clinic.

Pharmacists are kept busy filling prescriptions in the Pharmacy.

The X-ray is used frequently to diagnose chest and abdomen troubles.

Shown below: X-raying the teeth in the Dental Clinic; lower, the feet get medical care in the Foot Clinic.

Nurse . . . come hold my hand. . . .

Top-ranking medical men are doing a fine job guarding the health of soldiers at Bowman Field. Equipment used is the finest that can be obtained.

Pictured are medical and dental care snapshots at the base in 1943–1944. Well-rounded care was the norm. In February 1941, a few cases of mumps and measles broke out at Bowman Field that hospital staff handled and contained.

Wacs make excellent telephone operators at the Base Signal Office.

Sergeant Lorraine Kelly preens her new wings, insignia of the Army Air Forces.

Bowman Wac sends out vital Troop Carrier Command war messages on the teletype machine at the Base Signal Office.

Wactivities

Patriotic Wacs sign up for additional War Bond purchases as soon as they receive their monthly pay.

Pfc. Lucille Ferguson gives instructions to pilots in the Bowman Link Trainer. Substituting for a pilot here is S/Sgt. John Moon. Wacs perform all types of base duties.

"Wactivities" at Bowman Field were widespread since so many women served at the base. The duties and work details of the WAACs at Bowman Field are shown, and they performed critical services for the success of the base and its mission in the world war.

Wac Laboratory Technicians print vital Air Force training photos. Wacs assist photographers in routine laboratory procedure at Base Photo.

Sgt. Hugo Eberlein studies a negative which he has just developed in the dark room.

Wac Sergeant Stella Guhra washes prints. W have all received previous photographic trai at Army technical schools.

Photo Lab

S/Sgt. William Miller, Supply Sergeant of the Section, keeps the dark room supplied with photographic chemicals and other materials.

Another box of paper for making glossy prints. In addition to m training photographs, Base Photo also makes numerous prints for Relations.

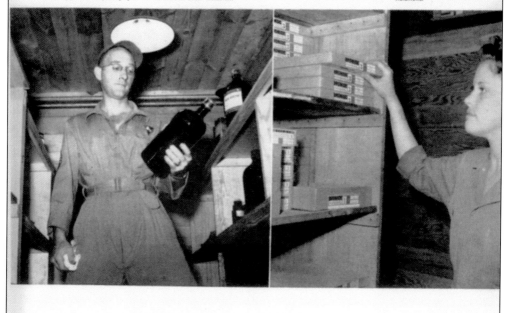

The photo lab operations at the base are pictured here, as well as supplies and work routines that were maintained. The photograph shop took and developed pictures of events on base, and several military newspapers were printed on base. *The Bowman Bomber*, *The Carrier*, and *The Special Service News* covered base news during the war years.

Five

BASE RECREATION ACTIVITIES

Bowman Field troops had available to them a whole range of social activities and sports programs. In fact, the premises were converted to accommodate various sports, and troops played games among themselves and with local sports teams from the community and colleges. They had a base lounge and commissary. The base generally was racially segregated between blacks and whites, and of course, women had their separate facilities. Troops played billiards and ping-pong and relaxed in reading rooms or a library. They had their own coffee shop and lounge. Airplane hangars were converted into recreation rooms and dance halls. Bowman Field had a theater built on the base. Troops visited parks and swimming pools. In fact, many were taught to swim for survival. (See U.S. Army Air Forces, *Wings Over America*, Louisville, Bowman Field, c. 1944.) Public swimming pools were segregated by law and by custom, and African Americans were limited to Central Colored High School's pool and one at Sheppard Park.

Fund-raising by local public-spirited women led to the purchasing of musical instruments to provide the troops with entertainment by those who could play. Mrs. Henry McElwain of Mockingbird Valley and Mrs. Ralph Strother of 615 Emory Road organized a group of 105 subscribers to donate $1 apiece to buy a new piano for the Bowman Field troops, and a band under Warrant Officer Wessel Poenie was formed. (See "Orchestra Makes Formal Acceptance," *The Bowman Bomber*, April 15, 1942, p. 1, col. 1–3.) Also many of the soldiers at the Bowman Field Army Air Forces Convalescent Hospital were former professional musicians and requested musical instruments they could play while healing from their injuries and sicknesses. Musical instruments were also provided to the African American troops on the base. (See Dwight Anderson, "MUSIC: Soldiers At Bowman Field Need Instruments," *Louisville Courier-Journal*, January 7, 1945, s-2, p. 8, col. 1.)

The 567th Army Air Forces Band under Warrant Officer Wessel Poenie played martial music and served as a marching band on special occasions on and off the base. It played swing music for military dances both for black and white troops and broke racial separatism practices in the military.

The Bowman Field Army Chapel was dedicated on August 30, 1942, with Bowman Field officers, dignitaries, and 300 people in attendance and the 567th Army Air Forces Band playing for the occasion.

Bowman Field troops cultivated Victory gardens to grow food. Apparently the soldiers could eat the food they grew or give it to the mess hall cooks to use for the troops' meals.

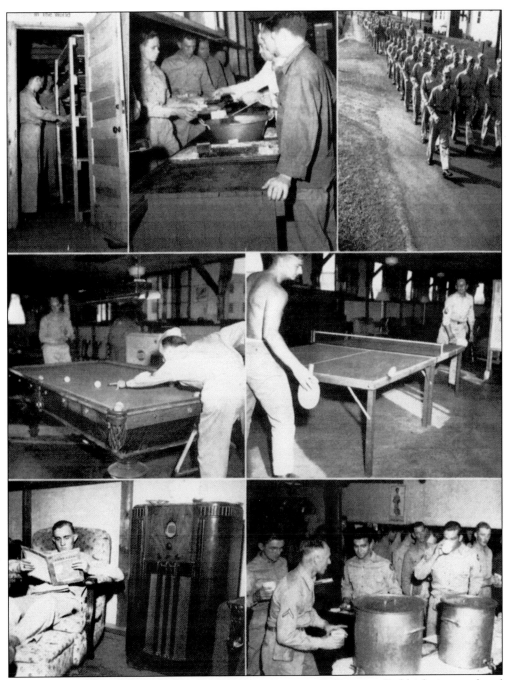

Pictured are soldiers during their recreation time, lounging at Bowman Field, playing pool and ping-pong, reading, relaxing, and eating. Bowman Field was fully operational by providing a full range of services, conveniences, and recreational activities and facilities. Thus, a sort of home away from home kept the soldiers' morale and confidence up during the war years.

The athletic program at Bowman Field is a full one, including, besides the regular training grind, all major sports, and allowing for various forms of recreation. Under the direction of experienced physical experts, the program is designed to build up a reserve of physical strength that will enable a soldier to "take it" as well as "dish it out."

★

Athletics

Wrestling develops that stubborn power and will to overcome an adversary.

he's happy when the pins are falling!

low: Soldiers take a refreshing plunge in the ol and (lower) receive a few pointers on ing.

The squared circle is popular with soldiers at Bowman Field.

Sports activities of both men and women in 1943–1944 at the base included bowling, boxing, swimming, and wrestling. Crescent Hill Pool and other local swimming pools were also available to soldiers. Swimming pools and parks were segregated by race according to municipal law in Louisville. Blacks were limited to Central High School and William H. Sheppard Park pools in Louisville.

WESSEL POENIE
Chief Warrant Officer
Band Leader

567TH ARMY AIR FORCES BAND

(Reading from Left to Right)

First Row: Technical Sergeant Elasic, Joseph; Staff Sergeant Brockman, John V.; Sergeant Bass Louis W.

Second Row: Sergeants Bernard, Morton; Cockburn, Alexander W.; Magnuson, Clarence A.; Miller, Thomas A.; Santilli, Victor R.

Third Row: Sergeants Woodworth, Emerald C.; Young, George T.; Corporals Bergdoll, Robert E.; Crutcher, Bernard L.; Saxon, Robert D.

Fourth Row: Corporals Schneider, Jerome A.; Turner, William H.; Vitale, Anthony N.; Wathen, William F.; Waughtal, Earl O.

Fifth Row: Corporal Wrocklage, Edwin C.; Privates First Class Bratanovich, Victor; Godfrey, Rollin E.; Jaeger, Harry A.; Nestel, Kenneth R.

Sixth Row: Privates First Class Ragland, Carl; Ruppersberg Donald P.; Sarran, Milton M.; Schor, Joseph S.; Schwartzberg, Jerry.

Seventh Row: Private First Class Wilson, Charles R.; Privates Herd, Walter W.; Orilio, Frank S.

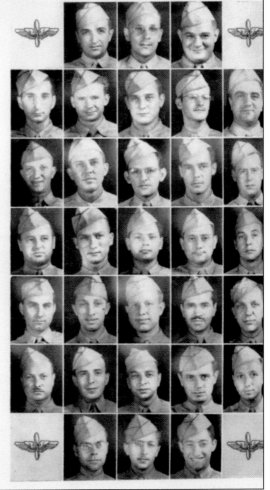

Pictured is the 567th Army Air Forces Band under Wessel Poenie, chief warrant officer and bandleader. The band played at both African American and white troops' dances at a time when strict racial separatism was the norm in many parts of the nation and on military bases. Bowman Field had relaxed racial policies that indicated that African Americans were part of the citizenry and a vital part of the army air forces despite racial segregation, laws, and customs.

Here comes the Band! Something stirs within the breast as the band goes by playing martial strains.

Above: The pianist of the Post Orchestra puts on a few fancy touches as he "solos" at the enlisted men's dance at the Service Club. Right: The Service Club is a popular spot for those who seek recreation. When nothing else is going on, there is always someone around who can tickle the ivories while a group of soldiers lift their voices in song.

Above, the 567th Army Air Forces Band is marching. At bottom right, at Bowman Field, troops admire the piano playing of a woman who is probably a USO girl in 1943–1944.

Technical Sergeant John Coleman plays dramatic roles in the weekly radio show.

"THE AIR IS FREE"

So says Corporal James McIntosh, announcer for the Bowman Air Show, a weekly variety show featuring all Troop Carrier Command personnel from Bowman Field.

"So, Dribble, you're in trouble again" . . . and off go Private First Class Howard Slavin and Sergeant Mitchel Stanley into their comedy skit depicting the ups and downs of "Sergeant Bullwhip and Private Dribble," on the weekly Bowman Air Show.

★

"It's the Bowman Air Show," says Chief Warrant Officer Wessel Peonie, as he raises his baton, and the 567th Army Air Forces Band breaks into the theme song of the weekly Bowman Air Show.

★

Here's a toast to the hosts of Troop Carrier Command personnel on the birthday celebration held in the Service Club. Shown cutting the cakes are Mrs. Freida Scott (left) and Sergeant Edgar Linder, Jr. (right), First Sergeant Andy Wilder and Miss Alice Kennedy.

Entertainment was an integral part of base activities. It included a weekly WAVE radio program that included band music and dramatic performances. Also, traveling USO shows came to and performed at Bowman Field during the war years.

Pictured are the barracks, mess hall, warehouses, racks and other functional buildings at Bowman Field in 1942 that made the base fully operational and largely self-contained.

Shown here is Bowman Field Air Evacuation Housing Unit building of the I Troop Carrier Command in 1943.

Six

THE 43RD AVIATION SQUADRON AT BOWMAN FIELD

The 43rd Aviation Squadron went through three or four reorganizations and names, but it became mainly known as the 43rd Aviation Squadron because of its community presence and participation in sports competition with local African American sports teams that they played and usually beat. Their uniforms carried the name 43rd Aviation Squadron, and the name identification stuck to the unit despite later official name changes. The Bowman Field base was populated by 3,277 men and women in a certain period in 1944. Men, black and white, numbered 2,226 or 68 percent of the base, and women numbered 1,051 or 32 percent of the base personnel; African American men numbered 243 or 8 percent of the total base population. However, many troops came and went, and the numbers fluctuated.*

The 43rd Aviation Squadron (Colored) was activated at Bowman Field, Kentucky, on July 28, 1942, and assigned to the I Troop Carrier Command. It was inactivated on April 14, 1944, and the personnel were assigned to the 808th Army Air Force Base Unit, Section C (Colored), part of the I Troop Carrier Command Operational Training Center at Bowman Air Field. On November 1, 1944, the base unit was designated the 1077 Army Air Force Base Unit (as the convalescence hospital unit) and Section C became Section F (Colored). They served to prepare soldiers for combat and nurse them on their return. The unit was discontinued on October 7, 1946. (See "43rd Aviation One Year Old: Squadron Boasts Fine Record in Drilling, Sports, and Marksmanship," *The Carrier*, August 20, 1943, p. 4, col. 5; *The Carrier* was published by the Dunne Press and run by military staff. *The Carrier*, July 20, 1943, p. 2, col. 1; U.S. Army Air Forces, *Wings Over America: Bowman Army Air Base, Louisville, Kentucky; Army Air Forces Troop Carrier Command*. Air Forces Division, War Department, Bureau of Public Relations, Washington, D.C., n.d., c. 1944; Letter from Archie DiFante, Archivist, Archives Branch, Air Force Historical Research Agency, Maxwell Air Force Base, Alabama, dated January 4, 2005.)

*The author tabulated the number of troops in their units from the book *Wings Over America*.

Pictured is a "Vittles for Victory" patriotic food and nutrition program at the all-black Beecher Terrace Public Housing center. On the right is Earl Pruitt, the manager of the Louisville Public Housing project that included emergency war housing for war plant workers. Healthy war workers and citizens who might also become members of the armed forces were crucial to victory.

Seen here in 1942 is a patriotic ceremony at Beecher Terrace, a black segregated public housing project. It became one of the projects to house war plant workers. The speaker in uniform to the left is William O. Willis, a painter, World War I veteran, and member of Peter Salem Post 45, American Legion. He served in France. Standing next to Willis is Earl Pruitt, the director of Beecher Terrace, and seated next to Pruitt is J. Everett Harris, another housing official. Fourth from left is George Washington Jackson, a World War I veteran who served as a YMCA officer at Camp Zachary Taylor and a Central Colored High School teacher of history and civics.

An African American U.S. Navy sailor in uniform attracts admirers and a friendly smile from a military police officer in Louisville as they stand in line for a train in 1944.

An African American soldier is guarding an airplane at Bowman Field. This was one of their duties, among others, and helped secure the base. These troops came from Hunter Field, Georgia; Fort Benjamin Harrison, Indianapolis; and Jefferson Barracks, Missouri. The men as civilians came from 10 states—Alabama, Kentucky, Florida, Georgia, Mississippi, Ohio, Pennsylvania, Virginia, West Virginia, and Puerto Rico.

Marguerite Stewart is standing in a doorway at Bowman Field in 1942. She graduated from Central High School in 1929, attended Fisk University in Nashville, graduated with a science degree in 1934, and briefly taught at Madison Junior High School. She became recreational director for the African American troops at Bowman Field after Pearl Harbor was bombed on December 7, 1941.

GEORGE R. HALL
First Lieutenant
Commanding

808TH ARMY AIR FORCES BASE UNIT

SECTION C

(Reading from Left to Right)

First Row: First Sergeant Coleman, John V.; Staff Sergeants Jones, Cratie F.; Manlev, George, Jr.; Sergeants Caffey, Isaac H.; Hoskins, Charles H.; McReynolds, Jack.

Second Row: Sergeants Mills, George; Parker, William; Wallace, Chester; Washington, Sam; White, Robert; Corporal Allen, Berl P.

Third Row: Corporals Brown, Joe; Brown, William T.; Caywood, Lee; Clardy, Nolen R.; Eddie, Thomas; Fields, John H.

Fourth Row: Corporals Ford, Willie; Graham, William E.; Hobbs, Albert H.; Ingram, Wade; Jones, Robert A.; Juett, Smoot.

Fifth Row: Corporals King, Eddie P.; Malone, Thomas E.; Mimms, Wallace L.; Quarterman, Henry; Scott, Elmorris; Stephenson, John.

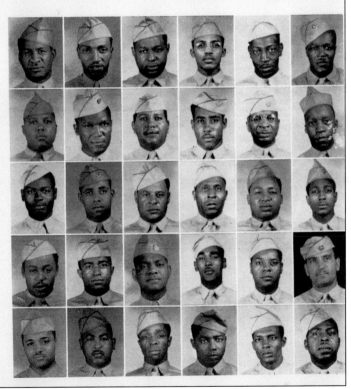

The 43rd Aviation Squadron earned a record for distinction for its service as a base unit. The 43rd Aviation Squadron was formally activated July 28, 1942, at Bowman Field until April 14, 1944. In the war emergency, they actually were at the field earlier. It became the 1077 Army Air Force Base Unit assigned to the 27th Base Headquarters and Air Base Squadron, 53rd Troop Carrier Wing. It served as a convalescent hospital unit and was finally demobilized on October 7, 1946.

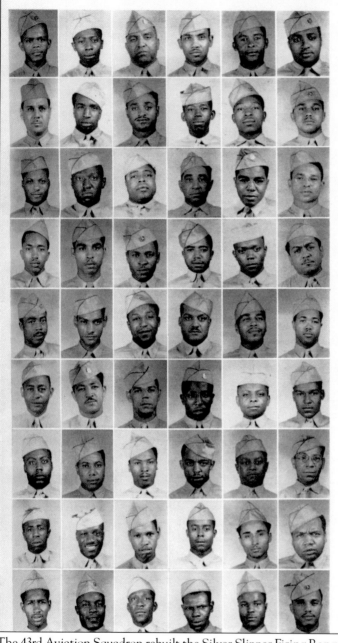

808TH ARMY AIR FORCES BASE UNIT

SECTION C

(Reading from Left to Right)

First Row: Corporals Tolbert, B. W.; Waring, John; Webb, Donald C.; Wilkerson, Frank; Technicians Fifth Grade Garner, Edward N.; Irby, William.

Second Row: Technicians Fifth Grade Jones, Alphonzo C.; Long, Melvin; Pickens, George R.; Valentine, Henry E.; Privates First Class Adams, Chris, Jr.; Adams, Marvin.

Third Row: Privates First Class Anderson, James A.; Ayers, James M.; Barnes, Houston E.; Beauchamp, Linwood L.; Booker, Lanier N.; Carter, Vernon T.

Fourth Row: Privates First Class Chambers, Fletcher; Clarke, Ernest; Cobb, Raymond L.; Cofield, Roosevelt; Cook, Earnest, Jr.; Crawley, Edward C.

Fifth Row: Privates First Class Crutchfield, John T.; Dandridge, Albert; Davidson, Houston E.; Dupree, Charles E.; Farmer, Oscar W.; Garth, James P.

Sixth Row: Privates First Class Gibson, James I.; Givens, Bradley J.; Greenlee, Rufus F.; Griffin, John M.; Grinter, Robert E.; Hairston, Ulysses N.

Seventh Row: Privates First Class Hall, Charlie C.; Hamilton, Thomas, Jr.; Hamlet, Harry C.; Harris, George; Henchey, Clifton; Hickman, Sylvester.

Eighth Row: Privates First Class Jackson, Jerome J.; Jenkins, Herbert G.; Johnson, Alex; Keys, William R.; Lane, Cary E.; LaRue, Charles L.

Ninth Row: Privates First Class Mann, Clifford; Mann, William; Meyers, Charles E.; Mitchell, Edward B.; Moore, Willie H.; Morgan, Limmie.

Ernest Westbrook

The 43rd Aviation Squadron rebuilt the Silver Slipper Firing Range used by the Louisville police so Bowman soldiers, including women, could train there. They served as orderlies for the Bachelor Officer's Quarters. They worked in the mess hall.

Seven

PORTRAITS OF SOLDIERS

The African American soldiers of the 43rd Aviation Squadron at Bowman Field were more or less eight percent of the troops that served there at any given time. The number of troops there changed as troops came and went elsewhere. Marguerite Davis served as the recreation director for the 43rd Squadron. She got cards, checkers, and other games from local businesses to provide the soldiers with games for pastimes. The Coca-Cola Company gave her games and cards for the troops at her request. Soldiers took pictures to send home, keep, or give to loved ones visiting them at the base. *The Courier-Journal* newspaper warned about reports of photographers over-charging soldiers desperate for pictures. Many soldiers took pictures in local studios, and some gave them to Davis as memory gifts. These photographs served as the historical record of their presence and activities at Bowman Field. The local newspapers rarely mentioned the 43rd Aviation Squadron, if at all. The formal record by the air forces archives, Diary of Bowman Field, is bare for all practical purposes. They apparently, did not mention the group and its activities at the base.

The group and individual pictures of the 43rd Aviation Squadron were, until recently, lost history. No one ever mentioned their presence at Bowman Field. Most people recall black troops at Fort Knox during World War II. Many of these photographs had been tucked away in a private collection of Davis, who died February 11, 2005.

Bowman Field arranged to have more bus services to and from Bowman Field so that troops, black or white, could leave the base to go downtown to the white USO or the black USO on Chestnut Street. They also could travel to and from the local parks and swimming pools, although they were segregated by race because of the apartheid-style laws in the United States. (See Letter from Archie DiFante, Archivist, Archives Branch, Air Force Historical Research Agency, Maxwell Air Force Base, Alabama, dated January 4, 2005; Two microfilmed tapes, B2060 unclass(ified) 1626 and B2061 unclass(ified) 1945: Department of the Air Force, Air Force Historical Research Agency, Maxwell Air Force Base, Alabama; Interviews with Marguerite Davis; George C. Wright, *Life Behind a Veil: Blacks in Louisville, Kentucky, 1865–1930.* Baton Rouge: Louisiana State University Press, 1985.)

These men of the 43rd Aviation Squadron are practicing close order drills in 1943–1944, which they became noted for by their officers and in public parades in Louisville.

A soldier is seated in a chair and posing for the camera. He, like many other soldiers, took this picture in one of Louisville's African American photography shops or in one that catered to blacks as well as whites. Newspaper stories revealed that some photographers tried to cheat soldiers by over-charging for pictures and warned them to beware.

In 1942, this soldier, Mussolino Elmo Garrett, autograph his picture and included the comment, "Loads of Love."

A photograph of Jerome Jackson is signed, "A Friend and I will never forget." This picture is dated July 11, 1942, which means he was one of he early black soldiers at Bowman Field.

This soldier signed his name as "M. Blackshear" and dated his picture "1-5-44." Note his collar insignia have the air force plane.

This is a portrait of Pvt. Johnnie T. Huett dated January 11, 1944.

This unidentified soldier is standing and posing for the camera.

Here is an army air forces soldier who signed his photograph, "Leroy A. Jackson, July 11, 1942."

Pfc. George Bullock signed his picture and wrote, "Thinking of you."

Left: This is another Bowman Field base unit soldier posing for the camera in a Louisville photographer's studio; his name and date are too faded to read.
Right: This Bowman Field soldier simply wrote on his picture to Miss Davis, "To a Friend, From Oscar."

This soldier wrote on his picture, "Lovely yours, Sam Washington, 43rd Avt. Squad, Bowman Field, Louisville, Ky." Note the picture's folder, stamped "Ghandi Photo Studio, 424 South Sixth St., Louisville, Ky."

Left: This picture is signed "Cpl. Willie Ford, To My Love and . . ."
Right: A soldier posing for the camera in a local photographer's studio is shown here. He signed his picture, "Jimmy Jackson, A Friend," and it was given to Marguerite Davis. Note Jackson's army air forces shoulder patch. The military encouraged soldiers to write letters home and to take pictures and send them to family and friends.

Here are troops waiting to go into Louisville's downtown or to the Chestnut Street USO building that used to be the Pythian Temple, a black fraternal organization. The Colored Army and Navy YMCA is located at 920 West Chestnut Street. Louisville's public transportation system detailed buses to serve the Bowman Field soldiers because of the large influx of troops who needed transportation to and from the base.

This is a guard entrance station at Gate Number 6. Soldiers commonly called the gate entrances that let them on and off the base the "Pearly Gates."

Eight

THE COLORED USO

The USO was founded in February 1941 to serve the social, cultural, and religious needs of servicemen and women. It consisted of six organizations: the International Committee of Young Men's Christian Association (YMCA), the National Board of Young Women's Christian Association (YWCA), the National Catholic Community Service, the Salvation Army, the National Jewish Welfare Boards (JWB), and the National Travelers Aid Association (TAA). The first mass meeting was held in Washington, D.C., on April 17, 1941. In five years, it attracted one million volunteers and raised $200 million. One billion people attended its shows and programs at home and abroad.

In 1941, the War Department asked a citizens' committee to help supply entertainment at training camps and bases. A budget of $3.2 million was allotted, and armed forces personnel were entertained by seven traveling shows on trucks borrowed from General Motors and specially outfitted for shows. The USO, the citizens' committee, and show-business representatives met in Washington and organized USO Camp Shows with the War and Navy Departments for the armed forces as a whole. This body was designed as the "official entertainment" agency for the armed forces. This civilian and military partnership organized and gave structure to the entertainment of the troops. It was essentially a civilian organization with military sanction to provide a service to the armed forces. (See Julia M. H. Carson (historian for the USO), *Home Away from Home: The Story of the USO*. New York: Harper & Brothers, 1946, pp. xi–xii; Eileen Southern, *The Music of Black Americans: A History*. New York: W. W. Norton Company, Inc., 1971, pp. 488–489; Laurence Jolidon, "USO Show Goes On and Over There," *USA Today*, November 27, 1987, p. 1-A, col. 3, p. 2-A, col. 1; Carson, p. 110.)

Louisville's Service Club pioneered the USO idea, and the federal government adopted it and the USO modeled itself after it. The Louisville Service Club opened on March 7, 1941, at 824 South Fourth Street in the refurbished Columbia Auditorium, previously owned by the Knights of Columbus but now controlled by Liberty National Bank. Thousands of soldiers at Fort Knox and Bowman Field frequented the Louisville Service Club/USO and the USO headquarters on Fifth Street. (See Joe Wayne Roberts, "Louisville Service Club/United Service Organization (USO)," (pp. 571–572), in John E. Kleber, ed., *The Encyclopedia of Louisville*. Lexington: University of Kentucky Press, 2001.)

Pictured is the Colored Army and Navy YMCA/USO building located at 920 West Chestnut Street in Louisville. This was the destination of many African American troops from Bowman Field or Fort Knox seeking recreational activities. The U.S. Supreme Court ruled on April 28, 1941, that blacks must receive the same service on trains that whites received, but racial separatism was maintained. In short, blacks should not have to pay a first-class ticket and then be put on a lower-class car because there was no first-class service for blacks. (See "Equal Service On Trains Won By Negroes," *Louisville Courier-Journal*, 29 April 1941, s-1, p. 1, col. 1, p. 10, col. 2.)

Pictured is Kenneth A. Morris, director of the Chestnut Street Army and Navy YMCA/USO center, with his wife and three children. They are probably at home in Louisville in 1942. His two assistants were Lou Alma Lankford and William S. Coleman.

Pictured is a copy of a page from the *Special Service News* that covered and announced weekly USO club activities for white and colored soldiers because of the system of racial segregation of the black and white races. This is page three of the January 9–16, 1943, Bowman Field issue.

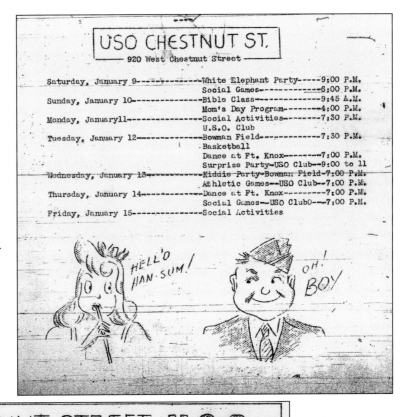

This Bowman Field *Special Service News* page of Volume I, No. 27, also carried the N.C.C.S. (National Catholic Community Service) and Young Men's Hebrew Association (YMHA) news from February 29 through March 6, 1943.

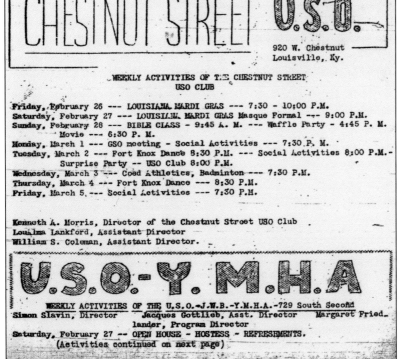

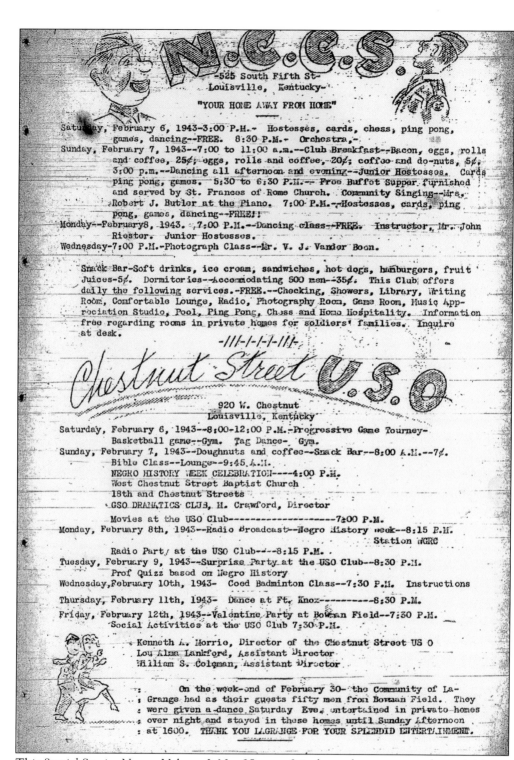

N.C.C.S.

-525 South Fifth St-
Louisville, Kentucky-

"YOUR HOME AWAY FROM HOME"

Saturday, February 6, 1943—3:00 P.M.— Hostesses, cards, chess, ping pong, games, dancing—FREE. 8:30 P.M.— Orchestra.

Sunday, February 7, 1943—7:00 to 11:00 a.m.—Club Breakfast—Bacon, eggs, rolls and coffee, 25¢; eggs, rolls and coffee,—20¢; coffee and do-nuts, 5¢. 3:00 p.m.—Dancing all afternoon and evening—Junior Hostesses. Cards ping pong, games. 5:30 to 6:30 P.M.— Free Buffet Supper furnished and served by St. Frances of Rome Church. Community Singing—Mrs. Robert J. Butler at the Piano. 7:00 P.M.—Hostesses, cards, ping pong, games, dancing—FREE!!

Monday—February 8, 1943. 7:00 P.M.—Dancing class—FREE. Instructor, Mr. John Riester. Junior Hostesses.

Wednesday—7:00 P.M.—Photograph Class—Mr. V. J. Vander Boon.

Snack Bar-Soft drinks, ice cream, sandwiches, hot dogs, hamburgers, fruit Juices-5¢. Dormitories—Accommodating 500 men—35¢. This Club offers daily the following services.-FREE.--Checking, Showers, Library, Writing Room, Comfortable Lounge, Radio, Photography Room, Game Room, Music Appreciation Studio, Pool, Ping Pong, Chess and Home Hospitality. Information free regarding rooms in private homes for soldiers' families. Inquire at desk.

-///-/-/-/-///-

Chestnut Street U.S.O

920 W. Chestnut
Louisville, Kentucky

Saturday, February 6, 1943--8:00-12:00 P.M.--Progressive Game Tourney-Basketball game--Gym. Tag Dance-- Gym.

Sunday, February 7, 1943--Doughnuts and coffee--Snack Bar--8:00 A.M.--7¢.
Bible Class--Lounge--9:45 A.M.
NEGRO HISTORY WEEK CELEBRATION----4:00 P.M.
West Chestnut Street Baptist Church
18th and Chestnut Streets
GSO DRAMATICS CLUB, M. Crawford, Director

Movies at the USO Club----------------------7:00 P.M.

Monday, February 8th, 1943--Radio Broadcast--Negro History week--8:15 P.M.
Station WGRC
Radio Party at the USO Club----8:15 P.M.

Tuesday, February 9, 1943--Surprise Party at the USO Club--8:30 P.M.
Prof Quizz based on Negro History

Wednesday, February 10th, 1943- Coed Badminton Class--7:30 P.M. Instructions

Thursday, February 11th, 1943- Dance at Ft. Knox----------8:30 P.M.

Friday, February 12th, 1943--Valentine Party at Bowman Field--7:30 P.M.
Social Activities at the USO Club 7:30 P.M.

Kenneth A. Morrie, Director of the Chestnut Street US O
Lou Alma Lankford, Assistant Director
William S. Coleman, Assistant Director

On the week-end of February 30- the Community of La-Grange had as their guests fifty men from Bowman Field. They were given a dance Saturday Eve, entertained in private homes over night and stayed in these homes until Sunday Afternoon at 1600. THANK YOU LAGRANGE FOR YOUR SPLENDID ENTERTAINMENT.

This *Special Service News*—Volume I, No. 25, page 3 is shown here—covers the activities at Bowman Field for the week of February 10, 1944.

The *Special Service News* published at Bowman Field announced: "On Our Stage USO Camp Shows Swinging on Down. All Colored Musical Revue; Torrid Tunes; Flashy Dancing; Rip-Roaring Rhythms; A Hep Band From Harlem. Bldg. 187 at 2000 C.W.T." This was page one dated January 2–9, 1943.

Page one of this *Special Service News* paper from Bowman Field notes a real treat for the soldiers: "A USO Camp Show: Broadway's Best; Straight From Harlem" and "Presenting SHUFFLE ALONG!" by Nobel Sissle and Eubie Blake, whose "Smash Hit" will be at Bowman Field to entertain the troops April 3–10, 1943.

Shown here is Pvt. Nebuchadnezzar V. Thrasher (left) of the 926th Quartermaster Platoon, who set the second bond sales record when he bought the first $100 bond from the finance officer, noted on page 4 of *The Bowman Bomber* on February 1, 1943.

L. D. Byers of the 926th Quartermaster Squadron was the first to buy war bonds at Bowman Field under new federal guidelines. He is from Statesville, North Carolina. Here Capt. Francis L. Linton, the base finance officer, is selling a $50 bond to Byers, who had been at Bowman Field for the last eight months. He said his bond would help to "slap a Jap." Byers's commanding officer, 1Lt. Daniel W. Austin, said Byers was thrifty and patriotic, as reported in *The Bowman Bomber* on January 21, 1943, page 3.

Nine

CHICKASAW PARK AND THE BROCK BUILDING

Some community and political leaders worried that a large number of troops would be coming to the city of Louisville as a result of the expansion of Bowman Field and its military mission and the expansion of Fort Knox farther south of the city. The military worried too that prostitutes might cluster around the troops. As a result, the Louisville Service Club was organized and became a model for the USO to accommodate troops, develop social programs and dancing, and chaperone carefully selected women to dance and chat with soldiers. The Louisville community leaders selected the Chestnut Street YMCA as the host for the Army and Navy Colored YMCA–USO activities.

Troops of the 43rd Aviation Squadron, under the direction of Marguerite Davis, organized wholesome social activities on and off the Bowman Field base to keep the men "fit to fight." The soldiers planned picnics and outings at Chickasaw Park, one of several racial-separate public parks reserved for blacks only. Pictured in this chapter are the troops at Chickasaw on the slide and posing for pictures to keep, give to Marguerite Davis, or send home to friends, family, and other loved ones. Troops also went to the Presbyterian Community Center in the East End or in Smoketown, bordered by Broadway Street on the north, Kentucky Street on the south, Floyd Street on the west, and CSX Railroad on the east. They played basketball and other sports at the center. Soldiers could and did swim at the Central Colored High School pool or at William H. Sheppard Park pool in the West End.

The Brock Building was named after Theophilus Clay (T. C.) Brock, a dentist and World War I veteran. The three-story brick building was a major location for dances and meetings, and it served as the Peter Salem Post 45 for veterans of World War I. Big bands played there and at the Madison Skating Rink. (Various interviews with Marguerite Davis by Bruce Tyler. See Joanne Sweeter, "Smoketown," (pp. 830–831), in John E. Kleber, ed. *The Encyclopedia of Louisville*. Lexington: UP of Kentucky, 2001. Photographs as documents and various citizens who identified people, places, and events.)

Shown are army air forces troops of the 43rd Aviation Squadron at Chickasaw Park in Louisville with USO girls for a picnic outing in 1942.

Here soldiers and USO girls enjoy a ride on the Chickasaw slide in the park. Picnics were regarded as fun and healthy exercise and were especially enjoyed if food was served.

The group pictured on the grass included Marguerite Davis in Chickasaw Park for an outing.

The Brock Building, 639 So. 9th St.

The Brock Building was located at 639 South Ninth Street. It was named after Theophilus Clay (T. C.) Brock, a dentist. He and his brother, Alonzo S. Brock, also a dentist, had a practice together at least in 1918. This three-story building hosted many dances, social clubs, fraternal and sorority events, and dinners. Soldiers frequented it, and the Peter Salem Post of World War I veterans met there.

Contract Blank

AMERICAN FEDERATION OF MUSICIANS

Local No. 637

THIS CONTRACT for the personal services of musicians, made this **7** day of **APRIL** 19**43**

between the undersigned employer (hereinafter called the employer) and **5** musicians (hereinafter called employees) represented by the undersigned representative. (including Leader)

WITNESSETH, That the employer employs the personal services of the employees, as musicians severally, and the employees severally through their representative, agree to render collectively to the employer services as musicians in the orchestra under the

leadership of **LOCKWOOD LEWIS** according to the following terms and conditions:

Name and Address of Place of Engagement **BROCK BLDG**

Date(s) of Employment **MAY 8.TH**

Hours of Employment **(4) HOURS TEN - TILL - TWO. WITH INTERMISSION**

$ 5.00 DEPOSIT WITH CONTRACT

PRICE AGREED UPON : **$27.50**

To be paid **IN CASH AT INTERMISSION**
(Terms and Amount)
(Specify When Payments Are To Be Made)

The employer shall at all times have complete control of the services which the employees will render under the specifications of this contract. On behalf of the employer the Leader will distribute the amount received from the employer to the employees, including himself, as indicated on the opposite side of this contract, or in place thereof on separate memorandum supplied to the employer at or before the commencement of the employment hereunder and take and turn over to the employer receipts therefor from each employee, including himself. The amount paid to the Leader includes the cost of transportation, which will be reported by the Leader to the employer. The employer hereby authorizes the Leader on his behalf to replace any employee who by illness, absence, or for any other reason does not perform any or all of the services provided for under this contract. The agreement of the employees to perform is subject to proven detention by sickness, accidents, or accidents to means of transportation, riots, strikes, epidemics, acts of God, or any other legitimate conditions beyond the control of the employees. The employer agrees that the Business Representative of the Musicians' Local, in whose jurisdiction the musicians are playing, shall have access to the premises in which the musicians perform (except in private residences) for the purpose of conferring with the musicians. The musicians performing services render this contract must be members of the American Federation of Musicians and nothing in this contract shall ever be so construed as to interfere with any obligation which they may owe to the American Federation of Musicians.

It is agreed that all the rules, laws and regulations of the American Federation of Musicians, and all the rules, laws and regulations of the Local in whose jurisdiction the musicians perform, insofar as they are not in conflict with those of the Federation, are made part of this contract.

The employer represents that there does not exist against him, in favor of any employee-member of the American Federation of Musicians, any claim of any kind arising out of musical services rendered for any such employer. It is agreed that no employee-member of the American Federation of Musicians will be required to perform any provisions of this contract or to render any services for said employer as long as any such claim is unsatisfied or unpaid, in whole or in part. The employer in signing this contract himself, or having same signed by a representative, acknowledges his (her or their) authority to do so and hereby assumes liability for the amount stated herein.

Name of Employer _____

Street Address **Captain Air Corps**

City or State **43rd Aviation Sqn**

Phone **Bowman Field Ky**

Accepted by Employer _____

Accepted **Lockwood Lewis**
(Orchestra Leader)

By _____
(Representative of Employees)

Pictured is a contract with the American Federation of Musicians Local No. 637 dated April 7, 1943, to employ the band of Lockwood Lewis to play at the Brock Building on May 8. They were to play for four hours or 10 until 2 a.m. with intermission for the sum of $27.50, to be paid in cash at the intermission. The captain of the 43rd Aviation Squadron signed it.

Pictured is one of the USO-style clubs for Bowman Field Army Air Forces African American soldiers in 1943. The hostess on the far right is Jeannette Porter, a USO girl and student at the all-black Municipal College. Her sister attended Wilberforce College in Ohio and sent the college banner hanging on the left wall.

Ten

LIFE IN COMPANY C AT BOWMAN FIELD

The men of the 43rd Aviation Squadron converted the Silver Slipper Firing Range used by the Louisville police for the First Troop Carrier Command. They landscaped the base for security reasons, built sports facilities, and provided for an area for Victory gardens. They performed orderly work for the Bachelor Officer's Quarters, and many worked in the mess hall. They also guarded planes on the base.

White commissioned officers, as a rule, commanded black troops. Capt. J. W. Hill, who commanded the 43rd Aviation Squadron, was a 29-year veteran of the army, serving overseas and in the States in World War I. He came from Beuchel, Kentucky, and he served at Fort Logan, Colorado, before his arrival at Bowman Field. First Lt. George E. Hoffman and Adjutant and 1Lt. Robert A. Nelson assisted Captain Hill in commanding the 43rd Aviation Squadron. First Lieutenant Nelson came from Colorado, and he commanded the supply and transportation problems unit.

First Sgt. John V. Coleman, a black non-commissioned officer, had been a teacher and athletic director in several Kentucky public schools. T.Sgt. Eddie R. Cummings was in charge of supply and hailed from Mississippi. He was regarded as the "Clark Cable" of the 43rd Aviation Squadron. S.Sgt. Everett Hayes of Georgia acted in the Bowman Field musical *All Clear* as the drill sergeant famous for his "delayed cadence." Sgt. Robert White was a 27-year veteran of the army who served as mess sergeant, and he was a former West Point cook. S.Sgt. James Leonard was from Wilberforce College and worked in plans and training, and later he was sent to Infantry Officer's Candidate School at Fort Benning, Georgia. Sergeant Charles Chapman and Nathan Hale were sent to Quartermaster's Officer's Candidate School (OCS) at Camp Lee, Virginia. They all successfully completed OCS. (See "Range Is Acquired For Exclusive Use By Base Personnel," *The Carrier*, Louisville, Kentucky, August 20, 1943, p. 6, col. 5; "43rd Aviation One Year Old: Squadron Boasts Fine Record in Drilling, Sports, And Marksmanship," *The Carrier*, Louisville, Kentucky, August 20, 1943, p. 4, col. 5; *Bowman Special Service News*, September 18, 1943, p. 4, col. 2; John V. Coleman, Negro soldier file, *Department of Military Affairs, Military Records and Research Branch*, 1121 Louisville Road, Frankfort, Kentucky, 40601.)

Marguerite Davis and six troopers are looking over plans as they built a base volleyball court. One of the major tasks of the 43rd was to help build and adapt the base's physical plant to military specifications, including sports facilities.

These three men of the 43rd Aviation Squadron played horseshoe throwing to pass the time and relax during their off hours. They probably built this horseshoe throwing range themselves.

Pictured is a football player who posed for the camera and signed this picture, "Much Love, Thomas."

These two boxers at Bowman Field drew large crowds. Boxing and hard exercise were encouraged as part of being fit to fight. The boxer on the right is Cpl. Ernest Westbrook, 24 years old. He was a finalist in the national Amateur Athletic Program tournament in Boston and the light-heavyweight winner in Ohio for the Golden Gloves, but he lost the next bout in Chicago.

Pictured is the 43rd Aviation Squadron basketball team with their trophy for winning the Fall City Negro League championship in 1942 under the leadership of Cpl. Charles B. Jones. Holding the trophy is Cpl. Ernest Westbrook, also a boxer. They played at the YMCA, the Presbyterian Community Center at 760 South Hancock Street, Central High School, and Kentucky State College.

A soldier is playing piano, and part of a drum is visible on his left. The recreation director and the Bowman Field base sent out public requests for donations of musical instruments and held fund-raisers to purchase instruments for the troops to play. (See "There'll Be Music In The Air (Force)," *Louisville Courier-Journal*, April 14, 1942, s-2, p. 3, col. 3–6.)

Bowman Field Building No. 187 was used for recreation and dances. Pictured are USO girls and soldiers performing the grand march dance. It was learned by Marguerite Davis in the 1920s at the Chestnut Street Pythian Building and taught by Sylvester Hurley, who learned it during World War I and became a dance instructor for African Americans. He worked at the Louisville & Nashville Railroad for many years. During World War II, he prevailed on the L&N Railroad to set up a USO lounge on the second floor for African American troops in those days of rigid racial segregation.

The Kiddie Ball (where attendants dress like kids) was held at Bowman Field at the Base Recreation Hall on Wednesday, January 13, 1943, for the 43rd Aviation Squadron and the 926th Quartermaster Transportation Company. Katie Brown of Louisville (shown here) won first prize for her original dress. Pvt. William Clark is her partner and Conga dancer.

Left: Katie Brown poses for the camera in front of the bandstand after recognition as the best dressed for the Kiddie Ball.
Right: A USO girl struts across the floor to be recognized for her unique dress and hairstyle at a dance in Building 187.

Marguerite Davis, the Bowman Field recreation director for the 43rd Aviation Squadron, poses for the camera with a soldier while the 567th Army Air Forces Band of Bowman Field actively played. This was the formal and all-white-member band for the base that Davis requested and had play for the black dances. Note the jukebox to the left. The owner of the Top Hat nightclub in Louisville, Robert "Rivers" Williams, supplied it free of charge until it was broken into several times for the coins and he simply took it back.

Marguerite Davis and sergeants are seen here at a dance at Building No. 187.

This is a group picture of the 43rd Aviation Squadron's sergeants and their commanding officer in 1943 on stage posing for the camera with the 567th Army Air Forces Band of Bowman Field. This pattern of getting all or nearly all of the soldiers and USO girls on stage or a strut across the dance floor was designed to give recognition and appreciation and to build morale and enthusiasm for both soldiers and USO girls. It worked.

Two jitterbug dancers are in full swing. Note the 567th Army Air Forces Band actively playing while black soldiers and USO girls not only dance but are standing behind the bandstand and chatting. For some, it was happy times, happy feet, and happy music.

These two jitterbug dancers won the dance contest; the soldier received a carton of Camel cigarettes and the USO girl seems to have a box of candy. Often these were donated items from local businesses and a way to support troops.

The dancers and the USO girls were recognized in a contest for a queen and her court for the dance. Corsages are pinned on the girls by soldiers to honor them for their support of the troops.

The dance queen is given a large bouquet of flowers at Recreation Building No. 187 at Bowman Field.

Some soldiers married local women as pictured here. Recreation director Marguerite Davis managed to gather up rifles to use in this ceremony normally reserved for officers. This is a marriage ceremony for a Bowman soldier and his bride in 1943–1944.

Pictured is the 43rd Aviation Squadron marching in an Armistice Day parade in downtown Louisville. These troops marched in formation with pride and confidence in Louisville, a patriotic city that welcomed their presence as black defenders of America and its creed of democracy, which needed expansion and to be fully embraced by all citizens despite race, creed, or color.